To AL:

A bit of ancient history,

Ha Eglehart

2/9/98

THE SHORT LIFE OF THE
ASTP

FRANCIS N. IGLEHART

THE SHORT LIFE OF THE ASTP

FRANCIS N. IGLEHART

American Literary Press, Inc.
Five Star Special Edition
Baltimore, Maryland

THE SHORT LIFE OF THE ASTP

Library of Congress
Cataloging in Publication Data
ISBN 1-56167-377-3

Library of Congress Card Catalog Number:
97-072032

Published by

American Literary Press, Inc.
Five Star Special Edition
8019 Belair Road, Suite 10
Baltimore, Maryland 21236

Manufactured in the United States of America

TABLE OF CONTENTS

THE SHORT LIFE OF THE ASTP

TO MITCH SPENCER,
who cared about the past

THE SHORT LIFE OF THE ASTP

Preface

    A substantial portion of these recollections about World War II were hastily committed to paper during a long New Year's weekend in 1972. The occasion and the impetus to begin to write was somewhat unusual. A number of times over the years since 1945, normally between Christmas and New Year's, I had called information for the area around Lubbock, Texas to see if I could locate my former foxhole companion, Jim Speer, who was not listed by the 99th Division Association newspaper as having been killed in action, as I originally had thought when he disappeared on the night of January 30, 1945.

    As previously, I told the operator that I was looking for a Jim or James Speer in or near Lubbock. After a long pause, the operator said that she could not find a James Speer in Lubbock, but she did have a listing for a Brooks Speer at Idalou, Texas. I told her to place the call and the voice answering was clearly that of Jim Speer, who immediately said "How are you, Ike?" before I identified myself. We had not seen or spoken to one another for twenty-seven years. I learned that he had been taken prisoner by Germans who came upon him from behind while retreating up a communication trench as our attack began. That, and the still raging debate over the Vietnam war that had been tearing apart our country, impelled me to write something about another war, not necessarily a better war, but a different one. The only "out" was a fairly serious physical disability or a farm deferment. There were no college deferments other than the accidental one of being in a Navy/Marine V-12 program, which gave you about a year and a half on campus, though your commitment was to become a naval lieutenant JG or a Marine Corps platoon leader for the final climatic assault on the forces of Japan.

Beyond dissemination among a few friends, who had also served, and members of the family, I had no thought of any form of publication until a friend from the Class of 1943 at St. Paul's School, the late Clement Biddle Wood, whom I had seen for the first time in many years at a dinner party given by my cousin, encouraged me to put together an article for the school quarterly, The Alumni Horae. The result was an article bearing the same title as these recollections, which was primarily a survey of those members of the class who had gone into the Army Specialized Training Program, the survey showing that statistically you were pretty well bound to have gone into the ASTP and then the Infantry, if you were nearsighted and had a score on the Army General Classification test at least ten or more points higher than that required for OCS. Because of manpower requirements, the ASTP inevitably meant commitment to the Infantry, and that is why three of our classmates never came back. Alan Hall, former head of the English department at St. Paul's and acting editor of The Alumni Horae, is to thank for publishing that article and a sequel entitled "Christmas 1944," which appears here. Thanks to Bill Meyer, editor of the 99th Division Association newspaper, The Checkerboard, many of these accounts appeared there at one time or another.

I must dedicate this submission to our former company commander, Bill Smith, 1st Sgt. Ed Orlando, both now deceased, and all the men of Company G, many of whom did not make it much past their eighteenth birthdays, like the replacements Gillen and Gutsweiler, who became my assistant gunners and ammunition bearers during the month of January, 1945.

ASTP SPELLED INFANTRY

CHAPTER 1

At the tender age of twelve, from a sheltered existence in the Greenspring Valley north of Baltimore, my parents shipped me off to a New England boarding school known as St. Paul's in Concord, New Hampshire, where, without then realizing the direction of the inscrutable hand of fate, I was carefully prepared for later service in the Infantry in World War II, which began a year later. The athletic program was non-stop: football, followed by ice hockey, and then, for me, track in the spring. The small handful that did not participate were assigned to something called "The Grub Squad," and had the pleasure of shoveling coal at the school power plant. In addition, there was a considerable amount of discipline with compulsory chapel eight times a week, and yellow slip inspections of the rooms, with selected seniors acting the role of future non-coms to enforce order and cleanliness. Finally, the academic program was sufficient to give us good preparation for taking the Army General Classification Test on which a high score, coupled with the minor disability of being nearsighted, would guarantee your future service as a connoisseur of Bill Mauldin cartoons since you would have all the qualifications required for the Army Specialized Training Program.

After failing the Navy/Marine eye test, I waited to be drafted. It did not take long. By early July 1943, one month after graduation, I had arrived at the Ft. Hood Tank Destroyer Center in central Texas in 110 degree heat for a thirteen week basic training cycle designed for the ASTP. Brune Levering, Miles ("Boo") White, and I had been inducted together at the 5th Regiment Armory

1

in Baltimore, and went by train to Camp Lee near Petersburg, Virginia for four days of shots, clothing issue, and constant KP. Boo had just graduated from Gilman School, but Brune had attended a Georgia military academy, as a result of which he fully expected to be tapped for Infantry OCS at Ft. Benning and become an Infantry platoon leader. Boo White was sent to Ft. Ord in northern California and eventually wound up in the 11th Armored Division, which took fearful casualties in the relief of Bastogne eighteen months later. Brune and I had a three day train ride from Camp Lee to Ft. Hood, Texas for basic training with a change of trains in St. Louis. It was sitting up all the way except for one blissful hour or two of real sleep when a porter piled up sheets taken off the beds in adjacent Pullman cars and put them in the vestibule of our car, which provided a soft pile to stretch out on. During the final leg of the journey from Waco to Killeen, Texas, a look at the barren fields and shimmering heat made one think of the French Foreign Legion.

That part of central Texas was very arid and dust seemed to get into everything. Sometimes when it rained, you could see muddy rivulets running down the window panes in the barracks. For the first month, we were confined to the company area and not permitted to go to the PX. The only thing to drink was water and a lister bag hung up near the dayroom, which contained both chlorine and a small amount of salt that made for a brackish mixture. Ingestion of salt tablets at every meal was mandatory. In fact, two eighteen year olds in another company died of heat stroke one day marching back from the firing range. Our status was marked by the weapons we were issued: bolt action Lee-Enfield rifles that had been packed in cosmolene since 1918. The non-coms threatened us with the familiar exhortation: "Shape up or ship out," meaning, if you screwed up, you'd be sent to the Infantry.

Contrastingly, as we neared the month of October, some of the nights became bitterly cold, though the days remained as hot as ever. We looked forward to Saturday mornings during the last weeks of basic because that is when we reported to the post theater to see installments of the "Why We Fight" series showing portions of "Triumph of the Will", the German blitzkreig in Poland and France, the Japanese "Rape of Nanking," and other horrors. It was pretty good indoctrination.

The culmination of our thirteen week basic training consisted of a two day encampment in an isolated area for instruction in hand-to-hand combat, the running of an obstacle course, crawling under the barbed wire of an infiltration course with machine gun bullets spitting over head, and crouching at the bottom of foxholes while light tanks rumbled overhead. We were supposed to hurl dummy sticky grenades at the rear of the tanks after they had passed over us. Considerable time was spent in instruction in the art of fashioning a sticky grenade consisting of a sock packed with an explosive, the necessary detonating cap and fuse, and coated with axle grease to make it adhere to the tank at the time of explosion. The instructor never explained how we were to find all the components for this lethal instrument under battlefield conditions.

The training had been thorough and rigorous, but we had not felt part of the real Army, as we knew we were college bound for an indefinite period of time. Our peculiar looking shoulder patches were supposed to represent the lamp of knowledge. Perhaps that is why we did so much singing while marching: "Tipperary," "She

Wore a Yellow Ribbon," "I've Got Six Pence," and "Swing Low, Sweet Chariot," - a favorite on a long night march, particularly when you had a good lead tenor to start the singing. Those summer and fall months of 1943 are the only time I remember hearing singing on the march until Sgt. Henry's platoon of black volunteers was assigned to our Infantry company in 1945, and instructed us in the ribald stanzas of "Jody," later to become the post-war Army's marching song.

The second to last night our regular army platoon sergeant, whose wife was employed at Baylor University, arranged for a platoon party at a hotel in Waco graced by coeds from the university. The propriety of the occasion was somewhat marred by the appearance of bootleg booze, unfortunately, consisting more of sweet liquers like Rock & Rye and Southern Comfort rather than straight whiskey. The effect on some, particularly me, was lethal, especially when we had the usual dawn rising, a hurried breakfast, calisthenics, and a battalion parade in the bright light of midday. The next day, most of the battalion loaded on a train bound for the town of Conway, Arkansas, located about thirty miles northwest of Little Rock, where we were to take a basic engineering course at Hendrix College. What ensued was an idyllic interlude. We were to take courses in reading, writing, and arithmetic of the trigonometric variety, plus basic physics and a course in geography with a focus on climate and natural resources, which might have prepared us for future assignments in Civil Affairs units. Nobody articulated for us the "mission" of the ASTP, but we were sure that the Pentagon had some special roles in mind for most of us.

In spite of the jokes you have heard about Arkansas, Conway was quite civilized. It was a college

4

town with a state teachers college on one side, and Hendrix on the other. You could even get the Kansas City and Big Band sound on the local jukeboxes. It might not have been Ivy League, but there were about three hundred coeds on campus, and almost no male students. The social system was run by the sororities. Rather than asking for a date, you waited to be invited to a Saturday evening sing-a-long at one of the sorority houses by one of the members. I was soon being asked by a senior, Mary Lou, whose father was reputed to be a rich planter down by the Mississippi. It didn't take me long to realize that my selection by this older woman was probably due to my rank as a cadet platoon leader. Though Brune Levering was made cadet 1st sergeant because of his military school background, the platoon leaders were selected by academic standing. At St. Paul's, my field of concentration had been scientific, and I had had biology with a fair amount of anatomy and physiology, two years of physics and two years of chemistry through qualitative. In addition, I was fairly adept at close order drill and marched my platoon to classes with a certain elan, which might have caught Mary Lou's eye.

Unfortunately, I was totally ignorant of local mores and of the power of Southern women when organized. I committed an unpardonable offense. After accepting at least three invitations to the sorority house, which was close to being pinned, I dated a townie, the cute blond who dispensed tickets at the local cinema. The result was months of total ostracism, not only by Mary Lou's sorority, but by all of the girls on campus. I was finally removed from this purgatorial state just as our interlude was drawing to a close at the end of March, 1944 - the ASTP, except for a few advanced physics students, was being disbanded to provide replacements for

5

line divisions. On the final night, believe it or not, we marched through the darkened streets of Conway to the train station singing "She Wore a Yellow Ribbon" and similar ditties that you could fit into a marching cadence. The girls kissed us goodbye on the platform, and we chugged away heading south for Texarkana and then a hundred miles west to a town with the improbable name of Paris, Texas, then home of the 99th Infantry Division at Camp Maxey.

The 99th's shoulder patch looked like a checkerboard on a shield, supposedly the coat of arms of William Pitt. It was an Appalachian division whose cadre came from places with names like Harlan and Mingo in eastern Kentucky, West Virginia, and southwestern Pennsylvania - add three thousand smart-ass high school graduates from New York, Chicago, and other urban centers, plus a sprinkling of Grottlesexers, and you had a large cultural divide. We had a platoon sergeant, basically illiterate, who stuttered when he got excited and sometimes referred to us as "STS monkeys." We also heard a great deal of the "F" word starting with the 5:00 a.m. whistle. All of us went through a second basic training cycle, fortunately this time only nine weeks. On our infrequent trips to the PX to drink Ajax or Pearl beer, practically the only sound we heard on the jukeboxes were endless, mind-numbing renditions of "The Yellow Rose of Texas" and "New Rose of Old San Antone." A week or two after arrival at Maxey, some men were culled out for artillery, engineering, and quartermaster units. To his mortal chagrin, Brune was assigned to a quartermaster outfit where he became a truck driver for the rest of the war, Ft. Benning an elusive chimera.

Surprisingly, in spite of my myopia, I qualified as expert with three weapons on the range: the semiautomatic Garand, carbine, and Browning automatic rifle (BAR). Eventually, I was made the BAR man in my squad, not as a promotion, but rather as a punishment inflicted by our squad leader, a staff sergeant from West-by-God, Virginia, named Howell. With its bipod, the BAR weighed twenty pounds, and when the twenty magazines were loaded with four hundred rounds of .30'06 caliber ammunition, you had a lot of impedimenta to lug around. Howell and I hated each other with an instinctive passion, and he had me on KP on Sunday, the day off, for many a month, except when we were in the field. In fact, he even had me on KP for two of the three days of the troop train ride to Camp Miles Standish below Boston in September. I think he must have looked in my 201 file and saw where I had gone to school, a secret I otherwise tried to keep from everyone, on inquiry mumbling something about having gone to high school in New Hampshire. The company commander, Bill Smith, was a hard-eyed graduate of Ft. Benning who only spoke to the old men of the company and totally ignored the rest of us.

About two months into this harassment from Howell, a manila envelope arrived from home. My mother had sent me a letter mailed to her by the commanding general of the Division, General Lauer, commending her on having such a fine son, who was one of the outstanding soldiers in the Division. This bizarre document, probably designed by some Public Relations officer for three thousand other parents, caused me to begin to fantasize. If not an aide de camp to the general himself, I surely was destined for higher things than Howell's squad, perhaps a staff non-com's position at regiment or at least the I&R platoon. As the months

7

wore on through unit training, live ammunition exercises, and maneuvers, the fantasy began to fade.

The training was strenuous with competition among the battalions to see which one completed a twenty mile night march with full field equipment in the least time, to see which battalion had the most men qualified for the expert Infantry badge, and so on. If eighty percent were qualified, the battalion was entitled to fly a blue streamer on its guidon. One day that I will never forget was when the battalion was engaged in a live ammunition exercise in the month of July before Howell made me the squad BAR man. Earlier, the platoon leader, a second lieutenant named Judd, had designated me as platoon runner and his general "dog robber." On the day of the exercise, the battalion was to advance several miles with supporting tanks firing their cannons and machine guns on the flanks while the platoons in very extended formation discharged their M-1s and other weaponry in the direction of the objective, some deserted farm buildings. It was my job to run back and forth between Lt. Judd and the platoon sergeant named Gilbeau, a regular army man, to deliver orders and messages. Gilbeau deftly ignored one of Judd's commands, which would have caused the platoon to move into the line of tank fire. 105 mm artillery shells were passing over head and landing on or near the farm buildings, which were blazing. The temperature must have been over 100 degrees, and the only way I felt I could survive was by stumbling into a muddy creek, removing the liner from my helmet which I used as a bucket to pour water over my head and neck until Judd sharply ordered me to rejoin the advancing platoon. That was a long day among many long days.

With the arrival of September, the training cycle had ended and days were spent crating and boxing equipment for a three day train ride to Boston. This time, however, we had Pullman style bunks to sleep on and racks for our weapons. Camp Miles Standish was connected to Boston by a commuter rail line, and we were given frequent passes to the city, probably due to our impending departure for overseas. Our main destinations on these outings were the Silver Dollar Bar and the Club Tic-Toc. I guess the high point was the night some of us went to the Tic-Toc with John Nelson, who had been a freshman at the University of Michigan before assignment to the ASTP. He persuaded a twenty year old singer named Lena Horne to join us at our table during an intermission, as she had sung at a college prom that he had attended the previous year. Our group was enthralled.

We boarded the SS Argentina towards the end of September and set sail from Boston harbor. The ship ran a long zig-zag course northeasterly towards Labrador and then southeasterly towards the Azores with a final run to the Bay of Biscay and Southampton. The Argentina had been a Grace liner, and there must have been almost two thousand five hundred troops crammed on board, the majority of us packed into the holds of the ship on canvas bunks mounted three high. Because of the number on board, only two meals a day were served standup style, usually powdered eggs for breakfast and then a supper/lunch of hot dogs and beans, as the most frequent items on the menu. Our position deep in the hold of the ship was somewhat worrisome since there were still U-boats in action in spite of the fact that the war against them had been won on a statistical basis. The entire trip took twelve days. If one wanted a shower, you had the opportunity to do so under cold saltwater, an opportunity most of us declined.

After unloading at Southampton, we were trucked to a D-Day camp called D-6 in the Dorset hills where the bunks only had straw ticks rather than real mattresses. In the daytime, we took road marches through the charming countryside past villages with names like Piddlehinton and Puddleton. At night, one heard the roar of bomber streams passing overhead on their way to Germany. One day, I was cleaning the latrine with a baby-faced GI named Goodnow when Ed Orlando, the 1st Sergeant, came in and said that he was mighty glad to see two Princeton boys learning a vocation. That was the first time we realized that we had a university connection, which eventually led to our sharing a room with Boo White after the war.

Near the end of our stay at D-6, the word was passed that one pass to London per platoon would be given out, and that it was up to us to decide who the lucky recipient would be. The consensus among our three squads was to cut a deck of cards, and I drew the ace of spades, which was the high card. Armed with proper documentation, four of us boarded a packed train at Dorchester with standing room only in the aisles for the long ride into Waterloo Station where we arrived in conditions of total blackout. Somehow we found our way to the Underground and arrived at Piccadilly Circus where the main hazard was to thread our way through the Victory girls, teenagers from east London plying their trade. We had just enough time to get into a local pub for a pint before the call of "Time, gentlemen, time" sent us back onto the street to find our way to the Red Cross hotel where we were assigned lodging. I had just crawled into a bunk for the night when we heard a strange

10

motorboat-like sound somewhere above us. Then the engine stopped, and after about thirty seconds there was a tremendous explosion some blocks away. I was so unnerved that I crawled under the bunk for the rest of the night.

The last night in England was on October 31, 1944 when I was assigned to help load 105 mm artillery shells on trucks at an ammunition dump located in an orchard. It was a night of an almost full moon. The last night at Ft. Hood had also been on October 31.

We boarded a much smaller ship in Southampton and made a night crossing of the Channel to LeHavre where we off-loaded into landing craft, which dropped us on a nearby hard shingle beach as the docks were totally destroyed. We loaded into trucks for the long ride to Belgium, grinding up a long hill on the outskirts of the city past a French woman moaning in a ditch next to her crumpled bicycle. No one stopped to help her. We spent the night in a pasture field in northern France under pup tents, trying to be careful to avoid the many cowpies round about. Though the newspapers assured us that the Germans were on the verge of collapse, our mood became more somber as we drove through eastern Belgium and saw an occasional ambulance coming back. We de-trucked at Aubel near the present war cemetery of Henri Chapelle and saw buzz bombs going over the hill where we pitched our tents. In the east a shimmering effect like heat lightning must have come from heavy bombing near Cologne. The next day, mail call was held on the streets of a small village while rain and wet snow was coming down. I finally had a letter from the Vassar girl I was corresponding with, which described an outing in Greenwich Village with 4-F type dates where everybody had a simply wonderful time smoking their first joints.

The rain caused the ink to begin to run and I crumpled the letter and let it drop into the rainwater of a nearby gutter. A great send-off for the front!

A QUIET SECTOR

CHAPTER 2

We were told that we were going up into a quiet sector, but there was still some apprehension as we realized that we would not be completely danger free. By the time we de-trucked at the edge of a forest of giant fir trees, we were in wet snow about a foot deep. Our Division relieved elements of the 9th Division who slogged past us staring at our new overcoats and regulation packs. None of them carried more than a bedroll tied with a tent rope. We were very close to the Siegfried line near the international highway that marked the German-Belgium border. The company took up positions on a reverse slope on the eastern edge of the forest about a mile from a town called Udenbreth on the other side of the dragon's teeth. There were a few artillery shells going overhead, mostly ours, with occasionally one from the German side. After a week or two, Sergeant Howell departed for the rear with a convenient case of trench foot, and his place as squad leader was taken over by Woody Woodward, one of the few ASTPers who had been awarded stripes. He had the fortune, or misfortune, to be hit in the leg by a flying piece of shrapnel from one of the very few German shells that landed in the area a few days later, his place being taken by Duffy, a gangly Tennessee hill farmer. Other than duty on an occasional patrol, the situation was not too bad, as we had one hot meal a day served a half mile to the rear by the company cooks, platoons going back in sequence.

The Division was spread over an eighteen mile front from near Monchau in the north to the Losheim Gap in the south with the 395th, 393rd, and 394th regiments aligned in that order from left to right with every battalion and every company on line as the front was more than three times longer than normal for an infantry division, making it impossible to hold companies or battalions off the line in reserve positions. The Division front was chosen as the main objective of the 6th SS Panzer Army on December 16, 1944 when three infantry divisions, plus the 3rd Parachute and 12th SS Panzer, hurled themselves against the 99th Division line, which the German staff planners expected to break within a matter of hours, permitting these divisions to form a defensive arc near Eupen and the 12th SS Panzer with its running mate, the 1st SS, to reach the Meuse River by the end of the second day. The position of our company on the reverse slope described above was almost exactly in the middle of what was to be the German attack. Within a little more than a month, hamlets, crossroads and terrain features with names like Krinkelt, Rocherath, Losheimergraben, and Elsenborn Ridge were to become the most valuable pieces of real estate in the world. We did not have an inkling of what was to occur.

The only bad time during that period was the day I was detailed to become a member of fairly large combat patrol selected from all three rifle platoons, including Ned Goodnow, who was in the third platoon. Our assignment was to walk through the dragon's teeth on a road towards the town of Udenbreth to see how far we got before something happened. Inside the dragon's teeth were a number of farm houses from one of which smoke was coming out the chimney. We had reason to believe that inside them were concrete pillboxes. We slowly crept past these buildings for a distance of approximately a thousand yards when the patrol leader wisely decided to turn around and withdraw. The fact that nothing had happened was not necessarily reassuring, in fact, rather eerie.

The first real excitement occurred one day when some visiting high brass went up past our foxholes to the top of the ridge to look through the hedgerow there at the German lines. They were quite surprised when a lone German wielding a Schmeisser machine pistol, known in GI lingo as a burp gun, began firing at them. They were pinned down at the base of the hedgerow about two hundred yards away, and I decided it was time for some remedial action. I removed my overcoat, took the bipod off the BAR, loaded one twenty-round magazine, and put four extra magazines in my field jacket pockets. Feeling ready for the hunt, I trotted up a path supposedly cleared of mines to the hedgerow and looked about as the visiting brass retreated back past the foxhole line into the forest. Another hedgerow ran perpendicular to it in the direction of Udenbreth, which I scanned carefully, but there was no sign of the lone burp gunner, who may have seen me and realized that he was out-gunned. My only commendation for this rash endeavor was a thorough chewing out by Duffy for having left the platoon area without permission.

One day in early December, one man per squad was detailed to go back to Krinkelt in the rear where the regimental headquarters and supply point was located for R & R consisting of a shower and a house to sleep in for the night. The shower consisted of a large metal barrel suspended over a muddy catwalk in a barn near a woodstove where buckets of water were heated. The barrel had a crude shower head fixed to it. A GI climbed up a ladder carrying buckets of warm water to replenish the supply in the barrel, and you stood on the duckboard and pulled a lanyard to get your shower.

15

Understandably, the water temperature was somewhat uncertain, and the air was definitely chilly as the cow barn was open at both ends. That was my first contact with soap and water since leaving camp D-6 the first of November. The next opportunity occurred more than a month later. At least it afforded an opportunity to luxuriate in a featherbed for the night in one of the local houses. Krinkelt and the neighboring village of Rocherath were soon to become the location of some of the most savage fighting of WWII. When we were there, the only combat activity were occasional bursts of fire from an anti-aircraft unit trying to down a buzz bomb flying towards Liege or Antwerp.

Around the end of the first week in December, we rotated off the line to a reserve position where we occupied dugouts with log roofs. We were briefed on a new assignment - an advance through a very hilly, even mountainous, area to try to take the town of Schmidt near the dams controlling the Roer River. As an incentive for this endeavor, we were told that there would be houses in the town of Schmidt that we could occupy. After suffering from a severe case of diarrhea for forty-eight hours, I recovered in enough time for this new adventure.

REMEMBERING THE BULGE

CHAPTER 3

Our battalion had been taken off the line in front of Udenbreth shortly before December 13, 1944, and moved back into the reserve area before joining the 395th regimental combat team that was assigned to the right flank of the 2nd Division regiments attacking towards the pillbox complex at the Wahlerscheid Crossroads in an effort to take the Roer River dams that controlled the river level in front of the 9th Army divisions to the north.

On the morning of the 13th, after chow, we packed our bedrolls, tied them with tent ropes and saddled up: bedrolls slung over the shoulder ready to be dropped in the event of enemy contact, C and K rations, canteens, entrenching tools, four hundred rounds of ammunition, grenades and our weapons - fifty to sixty pounds a piece. With me were my two assistant gunners and ammunition bearers, Don Riddle (not his real name) and Headley, a diminutive West Virginian.

Riddle had several handicaps as a soldier. First, he was the proverbial "sad sack" depicted in wartime cartoons. Of a gangly and unathletic appearance, he could never get his uniform right in training. Before we were issued combat boots, we wore canvas leggings. Several times he put them on with the hooks on the inside of the calf rather than the outside, which caused him to fall sprawling to the parade ground on at least one occasion to our considerable amusement. Don's other handicap was psychological. Though few of us were inclined to indulge in any heroics and only sought survival, he had a theory that the war was not justified. It was not a question of Hitler's policies at all, but rather a struggle between the capitalist powers for raw materials, particularly oil. A former ASTPer like me, he had been a budding geologist with several semesters at Penn State. He was firmly convinced that this was all that the war was about, and as we will see, this mental burden finally caused him to come apart.

All I can remember now is muddy trails and a seemingly endless climb. At one point, our Irish Catholic regimental chaplain stationed himself by the trail blessing each man as he went by - an ominous sign. We bedded down for the night on a steep hillside almost clear of snow in deep piles of pine needles that seemed as soft as eiderdown in our exhaustion. The following morning, we reached a deep gorge with a swiftly running mountain stream. Somehow engineers had gotten there by another route and built a suspension bridge over the water. Jeeps had brought up the battalion's supplies for the offensive, and crates were stacked under the trees by the water. Everything was to be hand-carried from this point up a mountain slope so steep that ropes had been tied from tree to tree along the steepest part of the ascent to enable us to struggle up with the equipment. Every man had to take extra bandoleers of ammunition or team up with a buddy to carry cases of explosives for the pillboxes, machine gun ammunition, or cases of rations in addition to our own equipment and weapons. After the first five hundred feet, the incline leveled off somewhat, and we found ourselves breathing easier in a slow, cautious approach towards a part of the forest where we could see more light indicating a wide firebreak to the east. It was about 3:00 p.m. - another hour or so of light - we were nearing our objective.

Sgt. Duffy was at the point of our squad advance. Our platoon scout, Figge, a nineteen year old ASTPer from Brooklyn, was far ahead. Behind him the platoon was led by Sgt. Standish, nicknamed the "Desert Rat," a man from Arizona or New Mexico, who looked like a skinny fugitive from Death Valley. A forty year old regular, he had been a private first class for years until the withdrawal of many of the old men from the Division to form replacements for the Infantry units going into Normandy had given him an unexpected promotion to platoon sergeant.

When we were within one hundred yards of the firebreak, a sudden burst of machine gun fire flashed green tracer bullets across the clearing in our direction about two feet off the ground: "Hit the deck, fire and movement, creep and crawl!" We were soon scuttling in a crab-like movement to our left to a position at an elbow formed by a sharp right angle turn in the firebreak which ran directly east from that point on, our extra burdens dropped on the forest floor to be retrieved later. Somehow we had all managed to follow Duffy who in turn had followed someone else under the machine gun fire to our assigned positions from which we were supposed to have taken the pillboxes in a surprise assault the following day. The opportunity had vanished.

There had been casualties: Sgt. Standish, arthritic and unable to keep his rear down while crawling had been shot through the buttocks. Headley disappeared, never to be seen again, leaving Riddle and me with only two-thirds of the loaded magazines for the BAR. We never knew whether he had been killed, wounded, or had headed west to find a healthier environment. The green tracer fire continued to flash overhead through the dusk as we frantically scraped at the frozen ground with our entrenching tools. I got a shallow grave-like depression about six inches deep before I fell asleep. Others continued digging through the night. After an hour or two, I awoke and continued my labors, finally hitting unfrozen, sandy soil. By daybreak, our positions were five feet deep and covered with heavy tree limbs and camouflaged with smaller branches. Don Riddle had dug his own hole about twenty feet away, and I kept wondering how I would get the extra ammo clips from him if I needed them. Daybreak also brought heavy mortar fire from the German positions across the firebreak. I can remember a heavy machine gunner in a foxhole to my left dropping like a stone, with a tiny hole in his forehead from a tree burst directly overhead, and the cry for "medic - medic" was heard increasingly throughout the day. Despite these hazards, we expressed silent prayers of relief for our company had not been given orders to attack the pillboxes. Word came down that a company from the 395th had already taken several pillboxes and that the 2nd Division was on schedule in the drive for the Wahlerscheid Crossroads, beyond which the fortified belt thinned out nearer the dams. The cheering word was passed that "Smitty," our company commander, had shot a deer that was soon to be prepared for a company venison dinner by the cooks back at the bridge. The promise became more tangible when Duffy detailed me with three men from the other platoons to carry the carcass down the mountainside slung with tent ropes on a tree branch. By the time we got back the mortaring had stopped, and it looked as if we were there to stay awhile. We scraped more dirt onto our foxhole roofs and bedded down for the night. It was December 15th.

At that time of year in the Ardennes, daylight did not arrive until about 7:00 a.m. It must have been about 5:00 a.m. when the ground started shaking. There did not seem to be a lot of noise - or maybe the explosions were so overwhelming that you couldn't distinguish the sound and only noticed the ground tremor that caused pieces of earth to fall from the edge of our holes and wake us up. The source of the disturbance seemed to be to the south of us - on our right, though at first the rumors started that it was artillery preparation for our own offensive. Certainly the Germans did not have this much artillery! As first light came, the roar of fighter aircraft could be heard diving in the same general direction, and it sounded as if bombs were falling. Maybe we were starting our offensive along the whole front simultaneously for certainly that would not be the Luftwaffe - but why were the planes diving so far to the rear of our lines? By daybreak, the thundering of artillery seemed to slacken and small arms fire took its place rising and falling in the distance from one crescendo to another. About 9:00 a.m., two S-2 (intelligence section) men from regiment came running through our positions with mapboards in their hands stopping at scattered foxholes to pass a message. One of them jumped into my foxhole and excitedly pointed at the map and then across the firebreak, saying: "There are two regiments of SS across there getting ready to attack. Those planes are Focke-Wulf 190's. It's part of a big offensive." As he hurried to the rear after this thoughtful fit of intelligence, I mounted my BAR on its bipod and waited. How many could I get before they crossed the firebreak and stormed our foxholes? I got the extra belt of magazines from Riddle; then changed my mind and got him to join me so he could take over the gun if I got hit. When were they coming? The tension was unbearable.

Suddenly Don said: "Everybody's leaving." Sure enough the foxholes nearby seemed to be empty of inhabitants and figures could be seen retreating through the forest. Somebody had passed the word, but we hadn't got it. We ran back toward the company command post keeping as many tree trunks between the enemy lines and our backs as possible, for we were now hearing the ripping, high cyclic rate of fire of a German MG 42 machine gun only a few hundred yards to our right. At the command post, the first sergeant, Ed Orlando, stopped us to join a motley group throwing extra clothing and odds and ends of equipment onto blankets and tying them up in bundles to be taken to the rear. Looking like gypsy washer women with our bundles we staggered down the mountainside. Near the suspension footbridge, we came upon a group of engineers trying to move a jeep out of the mud of a forest road. A German machine gun was firing high to our left at least fifty feet over our heads. At every burst the engineers threw themselves into the mud to our amusement, our more experienced ears telling us it was safe to walk by in a fairly upright position: "Don't be afraid you guys, they're only shooting at the tops of the trees. What's the matter; what're you doing down there?" one of our group called out.

On the other side of the bridge, the battalion CO, Lieutenant Colonel "Pete" Petersen, a little mustachioed West Pointer, was exhorting his men to carry a flame thrower to the rear. Cases of rations and ammunition were still stacked up. Determined to avoid our commander's eye, I ran behind a stack of cases; grabbed a half dozen bandoleers of ammunition, three K rations to stuff in the front of my woolen overcoat, and headed up the hill. I doubt that the flame thrower made it back. With the extra burden of the few bandoleers, the climb seemed to be getting to me. My overshoes were slipping, sweat was streaming down my face, and I was panting for

22

air. My companions seemed to have outdistanced me in the flight up the hill from the stream. It seemed I was the last man in the whole battalion with the SS presumably pursuing close behind. I stumbled and cursed and started to throw the bandoleers off, but held myself back. In some idiotic way, they were my only emblem of acquittal from this cowardly retreat - I was still doing something for the unit. The overcoat seemed to weigh a hundred pounds and hampered every movement, but it was my extra blanket for the night. The BAR was part of my personality, my reason for existence. Without it, I would practically be a deserter; so the heavy laden flight went on. I lost all visible contact with the unit, but followed the general direction of our approach march. By nightfall, I found the company CP with "Smitty," 1st Sgt. Orlando, and the weapons platoon with their machine guns and mortars - most of the "old men" of the company in faithful attendance - on top of a high wooded ridge. We scraped shallow holes in a circular alignment. No one seemed to know where the rifle platoons or the rest of the battalion were. I had had a K ration can of cheese and crackers for breakfast and no lunch, but skipped supper as word was passed that the company cooks, now in disgrace, had fled to the rear in the kitchen truck after abandoning their stoves and the captain's deer.

The word that filtered through the ranks from the CP with its still functioning radio was of a tremendous German offensive with five or six divisions including one Panzer and one parachute division attacking on our Division front alone. The throb of aircraft engines coursed overhead, and they didn't sound like ours. V-1 pilotless planes seemed to be passing over by the dozens, the raucous blat of their motors adding to the cacophony. At what seemed like the very base of the ridge less than a thousand yards away, strangely magnified by the fog and forest, came a constant squeaking sound interspersed by steady, ripping German machine gun blasts answered by the slow, ponderous chug-chug of an American heavy machine gun - tanks, German Tiger tanks! The mice-like sound was caused by the treads rotating around the Christie suspension. They must have been operating in low gear because we could not hear the engines. They also seemed to be far behind our original front lines and were moving in pitch darkness - some kind of infrared viewing device. A few salvoes of our own artillery fire fell near them limited to three rounds each because of the ammunition shortage. They seemed to have no effect, for the tanks were getting nearer. I began to shiver violently. None of us slept that night.

The Division's center and right flank, consisting of two battalions of our regiment, the 393rd, and all three of the 394th were slowly crumbling though they still held part of their original positions and had thrown the German time table off beyond all repair. They continued to fight on with aid stations overflowing with German and American wounded, attacking tanks with Molotov cocktails and firing mortars at 89 degree elevations to kill German infantrymen within yards of their foxholes. An apocryphal story filtered back in the next few days that one of their company commanders had been shot and killed by a non-com while trying to surrender his unit. The German Volksgrenadiers and Hitler Jugend SS troopers of the 12th SS Panzer Division, souped up on extra vodka and schnapps rations, attacked like maniacs regardless of casualties shouting and screaming in German and English. Our five battalions on the right flank held the front line for two days and nights while the 2nd Division formed a secondary defensive position around

Krinkelt and Rocherath. The five lost battalions later withdrew intact as units, but with casualties as high as fifty to seventy percent. The 3rd Battalion of the 395th held the extreme right flank of the Division front for three days against suicidal assaults by elements of a German division.

The role of our regimental combat team, according to the Division history, was to protect the right flank of the 2nd Division regiments as they pulled back to Krinkelt-Rocherath from the narrow gooseneck salient at the Wahlerscheid Crossroads over the only road, grumbling and cursing at the abandonment of their effort, due, they thought, to the inexperience of the 99th Division troops in failing to stem a local German counter-attack. They soon found the reality of the matter by the night of the 17th.

Our company CP group and associated stragglers like myself moved out at dawn in a southeasterly direction over ridgebacks that seemed to run in a bewildering variety of directions. I found myself marching behind the mortar men of the weapons platoon marvelling at the doggedness with which these thirty year old-timers carried the heavy mortar tubes, base plates and shells strapped in bundles of three. Smitty was near the point with his radio man and "the Top," Orlando, close behind with the company executive officer. We finally came to a peculiar series of ridges with pasture fields separated by hedgerows extending to the south. We were at the western edge of the forest and about two and one half miles north of Krinkelt-Rocherath protecting the open left flank of the 2nd Division. On the top of a ridge, I found part of the 1st rifle platoon. I liked this position. The ridge was so steep you would see anything moving at the base along a streamline. Moreover, the soil was so soft you could dig to a good depth in a matter of minutes. By the time my work was done and gun in position a non-com came over and pointed to a lower position: "That's where your 2nd platoon is." The position was much lower with no adequate fields of fire because of the denser tree growth. Yet duty called - I had been absent for almost twenty-four hours, and the BAR was needed; so reluctantly I folded the bipod; slung the bedroll over my shoulder and slogged down the hill to work my way around the perimeter defenses till I found the 2nd squad. Faithful Riddle was there with a full belt of BAR magazines. I felt somewhat guilty. A protracted exchange between an American and German machine gunner commenced on the east side of the perimeter. I dug in as rapidly as possible covering three-quarters of the hole with heavy branches and then throwing about six inches of dirt on the roof. Only a few feet on the downward side of the hole was left open, and the BAR sited to fire into a little stream valley. I had eaten the second of the three K rations that morning, and was feeling acutely thirsty. My canteen was empty as were many others in the squad. Artillery pounded in around Krinkelt to the south; rifle shots echoed occasionally in the woods and our mortars fired a series of rounds from their "pit" near the junction of two streams. By afternoon, a temporary silence descended on our perimeter and my thirst became acute - the stream gurgled by only a hundred yards away. Finally throwing caution to the winds, I gathered up other canteens from the squad and descended into the little valley with my buddies' guns covering me wondering what unseen eyes watched from the trees beyond. As I bent down to fill the canteens, I waited for the first shot to splash nearby; yet felt no great fear, as if fatigue and thirst had dulled other instincts for

26

survival. Safely back at the squad positions, I began to wonder at what I had done. The firing began again and the previous peaceful silence seemed to have been almost dreamlike - now reality had returned.

Suddenly the order came down to move out. We were to move back to Elsenborn Ridge five miles to the east. We filed past the battalion aid station. I did not realize we had so many wounded - also German prisoners in field grey uniforms and jackboots. We moved northwards out of the forest onto the Elsenborn plain, a poor boggy expanse covered with scrubby gorselike bushes - an entire regimental combat team on the march. The sky was overcast and fog seemed to generate from melting patches of snow and spread a dank miasma over everything. Near sundown it assumed a reddish-brown tinge. Jeeps and ambulances struggled past us almost hub deep over the trackless waste. Suddenly we halted and sat down in place - perhaps it was a rest break - but no, here came a long column of figures towards us out of the mist like soldiers in a battle scene from Macbeth. It was the head of our column, one of the two battalions of the 395th doubling back. Colonel "Pete" came striding by and emboldened by our recent experiences, I called out: "What's the matter Colonel? Are we lost?" "Jerry's got our radio frequency." was the cryptic reply.

It was believed that German radio monitors had easily penetrated our lax communication security, and using the Division call signs of Dakota Red, White and Blue for the separate regimental combat teams, had ordered our three battalions out of the line thereby creating a convenient gap for exploitation. If they had followed up their advantage, things would have been really bad. As it was, they were not too pleasant. It seemed that we moved around the plain in circles and

27

countercircles for hours as guides got lost and maps were checked and re-checked by flashlight under ponchos in the darkness. Being night blind, I was constantly falling in ditches and depressions, cursing in fatigue and desperation wondering if I could keep up. Over near Rocherath two barns or haystacks suddenly caught fire illuminating the scene with a flickering glow. Two tank destroyers suddenly appeared firing towards the flames, and figures near the fire casting gigantic shadows scurried to and fro. Artillery shells seemed to be bursting all around our column. It was a scene from the Inferno on a landscape by Hieronymous Bosch.

Finally, we seemed to be heading back towards our original positions and moved out of a pasture field into a dense second growth of trees with spent small arms bullets from the desperate battle in Krinkelt-Rocherath whispering overhead. There, unknown to us, 99th and 2nd Division men were fighting SS troopers from room to room as Tiger tanks roamed the streets and snipers fired from the church belfry. This was the schwerpunkt - the turning point of one of the great battles of the 2nd World War. We moved into the woods and fell exhausted to the ground. Heedlessly, without orders being passed, I laid out my bedroll and bundled up for the night. Fifteen minutes later the word came down: "We're moving out." Cursing and almost sobbing with frustration I tried to throw my personal belongings together and tie up my bedroll, which promptly came undone and dragged forlornly on the ground behind me as we staggered back towards our former position. As we groped around the familiar ridge line occasional shots rang out and grenades exploded, but I was too tired to care - I only wanted to find my foxhole, and I did too, hands groping over the telltale logs that seemed to fit the right pattern. With poncho thrown over the BAR at the foot of the hole to protect it from dank weather, I curled up for the rest of the night, oblivious to the sounds around us.

I was awakened from the sleep of the dead by a series of crashes overhead, and the sound of falling branches and trees. Shells were bursting at tree top level in a constant torment of sound that seemed to last for hours. I assumed a very small fetal position hoping to protect my legs from shell fragments. We later learned that our own tank destroyers were discharging a fire order that had not been or could not be cancelled. I believe our company suffered more casualties from that engagement than any other during the Battle of the Bulge. The shelling stopped as the sky turned from inky black to grey and I peered out. The poncho over the BAR was torn to shreds - the shells had been bursting very close; moans and soft cries for "medic" passed down the line.

I think something happened to a lot of us who survived that night. We began to hate the war and those we felt responsible for it with a cold passion. We moved out early that morning in the same direction as our previous radio-directed movement of the afternoon before, down a muddy trail to a crossroads near two battered farm houses, the road to the left leading to Krinkelt. To the right near a haystack at the intersection was a group of perhaps a dozen German prisoners in a new kind of uniform - a bluish grey. The men were very young and wore jaunty forage caps. They seemed to be smirking at our clumsy arctics and disheveled appearance. "SS" the word was whispered back. (Actually they were former Luftwaffe from the 3rd Parachute Division). I was carrying my gun cradled in my right arm and felt my finger involuntarily tightening on the trigger, and my

29

hand swinging the barrel idly in their direction. The moment passed; we reached the crossroads and turned left, a file on either side of the road. Suddenly machine gun fire was humming overhead followed by the unmistakable ripping sound of MG 42s - down into the ditches on either side - then across the muddy field to our right to former gun emplacements and foxholes dug by an artillery battery. The fire was becoming more intense, crashing through a hedgerow along the road and into one behind us. We could hear German officers and non-coms yelling firing orders about seventy-five yards away. The voices were high pitched, not guttural. Riddle and I had jumped into a hole with a foot of water in the bottom, and placed our bedrolls in front of us at the edge of the hole as if we might draw some last ounce of protection from them. Two figures from our squad scuttled towards the rear followed by our curses. Jim Speer, the platoon sniper, a rather phlegmatic farm boy from Lubbock, Texas, rolled into a shallow depression to our right. Cursing the clumsiness of the BAR, I unscrewed the flash hider at the end of the barrel; took off the bipod and hurled it away. Now, with the flash hider screwed back we were ready for swift, traversing fire. It seemed like the end was near. Seconds stretched into minutes. Riddle made instant cold coffee in his canteen cup and passed it to me while I tossed half a roll of Life Savers to Speer - our last meal perhaps. Figures ran across a hill in the distance; the range was too great, five hundred yards; were they ours or theirs? The hedgerow in front was only fifty yards away, and the chilling sound of foreign voices was getting closer. God, they were making a lot of noise! I set my sights with trembling fingers and began to track the roadway. Suddenly a figure appeared in the sights and my trigger finger tightened - at the last second I relaxed as something didn't fit. There was a black and white mortar aiming stake in his hands, and he was calling firing orders to our heavy mortars in very familiar English. Why he wasn't shot I'll never know, but the mortars rained down on the other side of the hedgerow and a temporary silence descended, punctuated by the moans of the German wounded and dying.

The immediate threat to the battalion displacement seemed to be over and we formed up on the road again. Field grey figures lay crumpled on the other side of the hedgerow - where was the rest of their unit? More spent bullets now flew overhead from Krinkelt. We pulled off the road again and marched parallel to the right hand side. We could see the church tower now. Some filthy bearded 2nd Division men - could we look that bad? - were dug in beside the road. One had dug up a frozen cabbage from a nearby garden plot. A humorist in our column stooped down as if to pick it up and had a bayonet thrust beside his hand with a muttered growl: "Get your own."

We turned left through a gap in the hedgerow, crossed the Krinkelt road and went through another hedgerow into a muddy field surrounded on all four sides by thick hedges and small saplings. On two sides of the field facing Krinkelt to the south and east were two platoons from the 2nd Division with the familiar Indianhead insignia. Though the steeple of the church in Krinkelt was faintly visible, our view of the surrounding terrain was non-existent. Soon we had the equivalent of a company entrenched on all four sides of this tiny piece of real estate two hundred by one hundred yards wide. Fields nearby had similar concentrations of men. "This must be an awfully important spot!," someone said.

Later we learned that Tiger tanks from the 12th SS Panzer Division had wiped out an entire 2nd Division company in their foxholes only a few fields away. Lieutenant Herring placed each one of us to cover the road. My position was at a slight bend where I could look straight up and see buildings at the edge of the village. I noticed the hedgerow in front of me was newly torn and shredded, pieces of twigs and branches lying everywhere. I prudently drew back a few paces; so the enemy gunner could not see me and started digging as rapidly as possible. Dirt flew as we sought safety in mother earth. A pile of boxes for artillery shells nearby provided boards for the foxhole covers. Because of lack of time, we dug shallow holes that we could lie down in and covered all but a few feet at the foot with boards, branches, and dirt. We figured that three or four inches of dirt might cause incoming mortar shells to detonate before penetrating our flimsy cover. There was nothing to do about the exposed portion left open for aiming weapons, but on a square foot basis we felt we had increased our chances of survival four-fold.

A command car skidded to a stop in the road beside me, its antennas whipping back and forth. The radio crackled out an unintelligible gibberish that seemed to suddenly galvanize the occupants into flight to the rear. They must have heard something they didn't like. A German machine gunner opened up to our east and bullets flew overhead. Three 2nd Division men without a spoken command jumped out of their holes clutching grenades and crawled through the hedgerow in the direction of the fire. A few minutes later, four or five explosions marked their grenade attack - the gun fell silent.

A brief whisper filled the air followed a fraction of a second later by ear shattering crashes and geysers of dirt all along our line - incoming mortars! I could feel dirt and branches raining into my hole. The bursts walked across the road and then back again minute after minute. Finally the barrage ended. I hesitantly peered out. The sun that we had not seen for days must have begun to set, for a dull russet color tinged the foggy atmosphere. It was as if this was the way the world would look for eternity. What was happening in Krinkelt? That short distance of perhaps a half a mile seemed an infinity of space - every step nearer a step towards the abyss, a fear-filled terra incognita.

This was logging and dairy farming country, and decent roads were few and far between. On this part of the front the dirt road through Krinkelt and Rocherath provided the only way to Elsenborn, the Division rear, and the main highway north to Eupen, Verviers and the Aachen highway that supplied the thirty Divisions packed into the Roer River front below the British and Canadian armies in Holland. Though we were not thinking of these weighty factors, but only of surviving from one hour to the next, there was a general understanding of the importance of Elsenborn and the long ridge dominating the marshy heath in front of it. Trucks and tracked vehicles on both sides, including the giant sixty-ton King Tiger tanks were bogging down in the fields and the twin villages of Krinkelt-Rocherath represented a funnel for our defending troops and the Germans advancing toward Elsenborn. The position was much too hot. If only we would be sent elsewhere!

And then just at dusk as artillery shells exploded around all points of the compass and the telltale squeak of tank treads sounded above the din, the order was passed that we were moving out and to the rear. The first part of that movement through the pasture fields around the twin villages is a complete blank to me and has been since the event, as if I blacked out - I have no recollection of the march at all. My memory starts when we were northbound on the muddy road to Elsenborn, Krinkelt and Rocherath somewhere behind us. The night is very dark. Silently a hand signal from a lead scout sends us off the roadway into the ditches on either side. A column of troops is approaching fairly well closed up and walking with a fresh step. Equipment clinks faintly and the squish of marching feet in route step hurries by as muttered oaths are hurled from the strangers passing through: "S---!, they're running away again. The 99th's f---ed up again." We hung our heads silently without response because it was true that we had been retreating since the battle began.

The column past, we moved out again and soon were in the streets of Elsenborn, larger than the twin villages and with wider streets made for vehicles rather than horse drawn carts. Maybe we would spend the night here, but no - we slogged on out the north end of town onto the open plain; no pastures here, just the scrubby gorse like bush that seems to grow on the poorer soil of heaths and moors. There seemed to be more light from the overcast sky than on other nights. We were not under fire. The trip went easily. About midnight, we reached our destination - a secondary ridge behind Elsenborn Ridge. As we faced east, the Eupen highway was somewhere behind our backs. For the first time since the day we carried the captain's deer over the suspension bridge in the mountains, we met our kitchen staff - cheerfully dispensing hot canned C rations that they had heated in makeshift containers. We were too tired and hungry to be anything but grateful. I had rationed myself to one emergency K ration a day - little cans of cheese and crackers, candy, powdered coffee, and packs of five cigarettes each. In the afternoon after the mortaring near Krinkelt, I had scraped my teeth on my last edible food, a rock hard chocolate D ration bar. Others had not been so lucky.

After bedding down for the night, disturbed only by the heavy sound of American 150 and 240 mm artillery firing at our rear, we awoke to examine our new environment: a long grey north-south ridge dipping gently towards an indistinct open expanse beyond which lay Elsenborn Ridge and the attacking forces. The word was passed that our battalion with Division engineers formed the only reserves and the final line of defense on this sector of the front, if the battered units in front of us gave way. We were told that there were twenty battalions of corps artillery behind us and tank destroyers on our right and left flanks. The roar of the guns behind us seemed to confirm this report. The sky was still overcast, apparently laden with snow, and there were no distinct horizons, the ground fog and smoke from burning vehicles and buildings trapped by the atmosphere creating an impenetrable murk towards the front in the east. We had excellent fields of observation and fire nearby as the plain was barren except for only a few tall pine trees and low bushes. This was a position to defend! Our artillery fire soon provoked the enemy to respond with 88 mm flat angle fire - a shriek and a bang - and nebelwerfer rockets thrown in - with their shrill whining descent and heavy, dull explosions. We felt so relatively safe that we stood up in our foxholes and watched the fireworks. A shell tore into the top of the ridge near a magnificent pine, raising a geyser of earth that reached high into the air and fell lazily back to the ground - pure cinematics. Then a call went out for volunteers to form bazooka teams to hunt 12th SS Panzer tanks that had broken through. Following a firm rule learned in training camp, I passed the opportunity by and watched as several other company members moved off into the murk to look for the roving tanks. More hot C rations induced an almost euphoric state of mind. The next day was almost the same and with the following night, snow descended.

By the morning of the 21st, we had a snow depth of about a foot, and 15 to 20 degree weather to go with it. Our housekeeping was rudely shattered by sudden commands to move out and abandon our new homes. Canvas shelter halves that had helped to form roofing for our foxholes had to be shaken off, laid out with our single blankets and rolled evenly for a proper bedroll to be tied with our tent ropes. We had ditched our issue packs long ago. Endlessly cursing, I found that each time I started to roll the snow stuck to the fabric and rolled in with it. Finally giving up, I rolled up the snow package and joined Riddle and the other members of the squad for the march to the front, a lighted cigarette providing a placebo against the cold. We were moving up to the forward edge of Elsenborn Ridge to relieve the remnants of one of the battalions of the regiment that had withstood the main onslaught of the enemy offensive and had just held off another enemy attack. Parts of the Ridge had once formed pasture fields separated by low hedgerows. The wind was blowing and the snow beginning to drift.

When we reached the objective two miles from our starting point, the gaunt-eyed survivors we were relieving, many without overcoats or even bedrolls, scrambled out of their foxholes and filed past us to the rear. We were on a forward slope of the Ridge looking at an even higher hill mass that served as no man's land to the north of which there was a clear field of fire to the

German lines around the village of Krinkelt about two thousand yards away. We were told that the Germans had attacked twice across this open space in the last several days, and that the bodies of some of their dead lay in and behind barbed wire strung about one hundred yards below us. The shrouding of the snow provided us with an excuse for not looking for and removing the bodies. We were the forward main line of resistance with two other MLRs echeloned behind us, the Division front having shrunk from eighteen to three miles.

There was a carton of Pall Mall cigarettes in our new foxhole, and I found a mild source of amusement in the advertising slogan: "Where particular people congregate." We noticed that there seemed to be far more foxholes than needed by the departing troops - a sign of high casualty rate from enemy fire. The extra foxholes provided us with our first real convenience in days, relatively protected latrine facilities. However, movement to them had to be restricted to the hours of darkness, for the Germans were firing 88's at every figure that moved on our slope. Emergency calls of nature requiring a sudden daytime move to an abandoned foxhole almost invariably provoked a German response. During daylight, the shells screamed in constantly causing sensations of concussion and ringing eardrums. Frozen dirt rained into our canteen cups and C ration cans as we tried to heat them over burning fragments of waxed cardboard K ration containers. Our ears were so attuned that we could judge the trajectory of the shells within five to ten yards. Casualties began to pick up significantly. Two eighteen year old replacements in a hole ten yards to the left were killed instantly by a direct hit, and we struggled to the company command post after nightfall with a party of four dragging their bodies in blankets.

Duffy, our squad leader, was killed and Mike Kelly, a little bantam Irishman from Boston, took over the squad with me as second in command - a baton in every bedroll. Nelson and Sutphen had taken over the 2nd platoon - a buck sergeant and a private first class taking the place of a second lieutenant and a tech. sergeant. Lieutenant Greenough, our touch football coach from camp D-6 in England, had been carried away from the 3rd platoon with multiple wounds. Our platoon sergeant from Camp Maxey, the Desert Rat, had been wounded and his place had been taken by the platoon guide, a staff sergeant named Moore, who had left the mines to become a department store floorwalker in some West Virginia town before being drafted. He in turn was killed the first day on Elsenborn Ridge, and the platoon was taken over by Hugo Degamo, a tall Italian, one of the better squad leaders who fortunately lacked excessive ambition and was generally liked by all. The 1st platoon sergeant's position was taken over by a private first class from Joliet, Illinois, Bob Stella, a former apprentice machinist, who had been taken into the ASTP program. Bob later served as platoon leader when Lieutenant Womack was killed and was considered indispensable. He survived the remaining months of the war without injury as did my future Princeton roommate, Ned Goodnow, Capt. Bill Smith, 1st Sgt. Ed Orlando, and a handful of others, mostly in the weapons platoon.

The cooks still had not replaced the abandoned stoves, but sent us Marmite lined cans of hot coffee, soup and hot chocolate brought up after dark when the shelling ceased. The Germans were using direct line of sight fire with their 88's, and our artillery was responding at night with indirect fire patterns working from coordinates. After dark, our outgoing shells would create a familiar whispering, rustling sound above - sometimes so many that we would look up to see if some of the stars would wink out.

Following the snow had come bitter cold. None of us had shaved in weeks, and our hands and faces were filthy from digging and heating food and coffee over stoves made from C ration cans and dirt with gasoline or the waxed cardboard from K rations used as fuel. Our fingers were beginning to swell and crack from the dryness and frostbite. I could no longer get my feet in the leather combat boots due to swelling and wrapped them in blanket strips and hobbled around on patrol and guard duty in the clumsy buckle arctics.

CHRISTMAS, 1944

CHAPTER 4

It must have been Christmas Eve when it came my turn to go back to the ration point near the company command post to fill the squad's canteens. The trip went slowly because rival patrols in bedsheets and white camouflage suits were constantly penetrating each others lines, and the day's password had to be whispered from checkpoint to checkpoint. I made my way by the light of a half moon. It was so cold that the dry snow squeaked under foot. I had not bothered to screw the caps back on several of the canteens, which I was holding by the neck chains, and noticed that the water was already forming a thin film of ice when I stopped at the position of a forward artillery observer marked by a very large radio antenna near the hedgerow leading to our platoon's leader position. Far in the distance a pulsing pyrotechnic display vaguely suggested a celebration to the season: a glowing object at first almost white, fading into yellow, then cerise and dull red ascending vertically into the heavens. The forward observer said that it must be a shell from a German eighteen inch railway gun firing at high angle far in the distance. Hoarfrost glittered on upturned piles of dirt around the foxholes. It was like being on the face of the moon. I distributed the canteens and returned to the foxhole that Don Riddle and I shared.

We had not completed our roofing operation, and only had poles laid across the foxhole to support our shelter halves. Something seemed to be wrong - a dark form was bobbing up and down on its knees in the hole with a rope running from one of the poles into the darkness. It was Don, and the rope was around his neck.

40

He had slashed his wrists with a razor blade. The blood appeared black in the moonlight. "Let me alone, let me alone - it's no use, I can't stand it anymore," he sobbed. He had suffered the ultimate loss of faith. Nothing that we had done or endured had any meaning for him. I cut him down with my trench knife, bandaged his wrists and half carried him sobbing to the rear.

I pleaded with Orlando not to mention the suicide attempt in the company casualty report, and mark him only as a combat fatigue case, though probably Don wanted the escape that a psychiatric ward and a section eight discharge would give him. When I returned to the platoon area, Lt. Herring invited me to his foxhole to take some strong slugs of whiskey from his liquor ration, most of which he had already distributed to the men. Then solicitously protecting me from a lonely night on this bitter Yuletide, he got another ASTPer from Lubbock, Texas, the platoon sniper, Jim Speer, to move in with me. With reddish-blond hair, a round face and upturned nose, Jim looked like a Dutch farmer. A hint of country humor often played at the corner of his mouth, but I suspected he would never really smile until he was back on his cotton farm in the Texas panhandle. We stayed together on easy terms throughout the snows of January, shellings, combat and recon patrols, until Jim was captured and ten of the twelve members of our squad were killed along with Lt. Herring in the final drive to the edge of the Eifel Forest that we had left such a long time ago.

On Christmas day, the stoveless cooks managed to send up turkey sandwiches in cardboard boxes. The sandwiches had become frozen solid en route. Then a miracle occurred. Christmas packages held back for the occasion arrived for hurried distribution. The Vassar girl had mailed a leather picture frame with her own blonde visage set off by pearls and a formal gown. I tried setting it up at the edge of the foxhole by the grenades and ammo clips, but the formal gown was too much, and I folded the picture frame quietly away under my bedroll. A maiden aunt in the family, perhaps deceived as to the true nature of my military duties, had sent a leather bound, handsomely illustrated book on upland game shooting. But best of all was a compact package from my fourteen year old nephew who had been very ill - recovering from rheumatic fever: gloves, socks, a little folding stove with heat tablets, a woolen muffler and balaclava helmet that he had knitted himself as a form of occupational therapy. Somebody understood what was going on up here!

The German shelling had been intense in the early morning, but then died away as an American artillery liaison plane cruised overhead. The sun shone with real vigor for the first time in a month or more. The temperature was up to the freezing point. It was time for a stroll. I took off my helmet and put on the new scarf. After joking with the two men to our right about the Christmas dinner, I found an abandoned shallow foxhole only a foot or two deep lined with straw. I stretched out to luxuriate in the warming rays, but found that my head was bumping against something hard - it was the nose of an unexploded German 88 shell buried into the edge. I shifted to a more comfortable position and pulled out a little pocket book of verse and inspirational prose given me by my mother. I skipped over Mark and Luke to read and reread as a litany for the day passages from Epictetus and Henley's "Invictus."

WINTER OFFENSIVE

CHAPTER 5

After New Year's it became clear that our part of the front had stabilized, though there had been some final desperate tank-Infantry attacks against portions of the 99th and 1st Division lines right after Christmas. The 12th SS Panzers almost broke through the 1st Division south of Elsenborn at Butgenbach at the corner or hinge of the northern portion of the Bulge but were thrown back with heavy losses. A 3rd Panzer Grenadier attack was launched about five hundred yards north of the hole that Jim Speer and I were in on the night of December 27th, but they were driven off with heavy machine gun and massed artillery fire using white phosphorus shells - a fantastic sight at night. We stood to all night waiting for the enemy with grenades and ammo clips lined up in front of us, but they did not hit our part of the line.

These were the last offensive efforts by the Germans on our front, though fifty miles to the southwest Bastogne had become the scene of a tremendous battle with seven or eight divisions employed on each side. Clear weather brought relief from German artillery which greatly diminished as spotter planes cruised the lines as airborne forward observers. On New Year's Day the Luftwaffe made its last offensive effort of the war with fighter-bomber strikes on all our forward airfields in Belgium and Holland destroying over two hundred Allied planes on the ground. Their losses were even heavier. Some of them flew over our lines at a very low altitude as if curious to see what we looked like. We raised our guns at the ready as several ME-109s with black crosses on their wings made passes down the foxhole line, but no one fired when we realized they were only sight-seeing. The situation had quieted down so much that we only had to have one man per squad stand guard duty at nighttime, giving us the luxury of a lot of sack time in our foxholes stretched out head to toe. We were warm enough from body heat and the sleeping bags that had finally been issued to us.

Whole days passed without a single casualty in the company, whose ranks were rapidly filled with eighteen year old draftees straight from basic training, and men converted from excess anti-aircraft units. The demand for replacements was so great that black volunteers from truck and port battalions were being accepted in platoon units, though these did not come in until February.

Two young high school graduates from Ohio with an improbable combination of names - Gillen and Gutsweiler - came in to take Riddle and Headley's places as ammo bearers and assistant gunners for the squad BAR. Like most replacements, they had been together from basic training as a result of the "buddy" system deliberately encouraged by the Army. To have one friend with whom you had some shared experiences was infinitely better than being thrust alone into the strangeness of a new outfit where few seemed to care whether you lived or died, and so men were paired, often arbitrarily, through the replacement chain to the front lines. Gillen and Gutsweiler may have been linked together solely because of a juxtaposition of names on a company roster, but they were much alike and exhibited a boyish enthusiasm and eagerness to help that was almost embarrassing to those of us whose only humor was of the graveyard variety, and whose sole enthusiasm was for the reprieve of a non-fatal wound. I remembered that I must have been somewhat like that when we finished basic training at Fort Hood, though the indefinable hopes and expectations of an eighteen year old for a romantic military assignment had been finally ground away in the crucible of Camp Maxey a year later after the demise of the ASTP program.

I had a dual responsibility with Gillen and Gutsweiler: As BAR man to review with them the tactical use of the weapon and as acting assistant squad leader to give them useful hints for survival: how we heated our rations, avoidance of frostbite or trenchfoot, the sound of in-coming "mail," enemy habits, etc. In talking to them and helping Kelly brief other replacements, I realized that a great change had taken place. Jim Speer and I and all the other surviving ASTP group were now "old men" of the company. We had completely merged into the corporate identity of the unit which now seemed to be "ours" in the same possessive sense with which it had controlled our lives from Camp Maxey to Elsenborn Ridge. This was not the result of any patriotic fervor but a slow, natural process of shared association under extraordinary circumstances that had brought us to this state of grace among the elect without any conscious act of will other than the dumb, mule-like endurance and luck that had brought us to early January, 1945. Rank was unimportant. Few of the acting squad and platoon leaders ever received their stripes. What was important was when you had come into the unit, which created an invisible mark of seniority and expertise, to which due deference was given by the newer men. Home and country was another world, far away in time and space. Our life-reality itself was this time and place - our sole commitment, our loyalty to the unit. The boundary of our world stretched no further than the snow-laden crest of Elsenborn Ridge behind us to the German

45

positions at the edge of the Eifel Forest before us from Christmas until the end of January.

We busied ourselves with endless work on improving the depth and shape of our foxholes, creating makeshift stoves and going on nighttime ration details and guard duty. There was little movement above ground in daylight unless absolutely necessary. With pencil stubs and V-mail sheets we began corresponding vigorously with friends and family to indicate we were still alive and receptive towards additional packages. Most of my letters affected old soldier bravado, but I dropped the pose with my mother: Hershey bars, mustard, pickles, jam, anchovy paste, Liederbranz cheese and other bizarre desires plagued me constantly and resulted in endless entreaties to her for such delicacies, none of which ever reached the front. Our diet consisted of the emergency K rations, cans of C ration hash of a gelatinous grey, hot soup or cocoa, and occasional fresh bread brought up at night.

With additional digging in the frozen soil and further work on our foxholes' roofs with boards and packing cases scavenged from everywhere, we had become quite snug. We threw the spoil behind us forming protective mounds that shielded us from friendly fire in the rear in the event of a German foray. The snow on the roofs made for reasonable warmth down below. One day about the middle of January, when it was snowing heavily, the regimental commander, Colonel Scott, came up to inspire us with his presence which had not been seen near the front line since our arrival in November. The mental image I still have is of a figure in an Air Corps fleece lined jacket, creased pants and polished leather jump boots with two aides in attendance. As he passed down our platoon line, the filthy, bearded faces popping out of the holes in dirty overcoats to stare in wonderment at the visitors looked more like groundhogs than soldiers. He bawled out to Lieutenant Herring, "Those beards have got to come off Lieutenant and I want 360 degree, all-around fighting positions. Get these damn roofs off these foxholes. This position's a disgrace. You might be overrun at any minute and they wouldn't even be able to see the enemy." John Herring quivered but remained silent. As the Colonel departed for the safety of his command post several miles to the rear, Herring walked past our holes and in a rare burst of profanity told us what Scott could do; "Forget it," he told each of us.

Possibly one beneficial result of the Colonel's visit was the commencement of a rotation system to the rear to wash and shave for the first time since before the attack toward the dams. When my turn came, a party of us trudged back several miles along a road with huge drifts of snow on either side. This was our nighttime lifeline for jeep borne food. Elsenborn was the rear, and the inside of the stone farm houses, of which about half were damaged by shell fire, seemed like civilization. Scissors and two razor blades got rid of a fine growth of month-old beard with much tugging and scraping. Then into a barber's "chair" manned by a truck driver earning a few Belgian occupation francs on the side. The haircut was halfway through when planes started strafing runs on the main street outside. Our barber ran out to man a fifty caliber machine gun on his truck parked nearby, and the din was terrific. I was glad that he was able to return to finish the other side of my head.

We later learned that the planes were RAF Spitfires that had mistaken several of the new wide track, low slung M-76 tank destroyers with muzzle brakes on

47

their guns in the streets for German Panthers or Tigers. One plane was shot down. Later some of us crashed a chow line of a tank destroyer unit and wheedled our way past a benevolent mess sergeant to a feast of pancakes, bacon and powdered milk that we devoured like starving street urchins. We spent the night in the total security of deep covered log bunkers at Camp Elsenborn in the woods east of town, a former Belgian army training center. Here we saw for the first time the long heralded miracle of American industry designed to prevent frozen feet - the Shoe Pac. We found it being worn by most of the rear echelon troops, including some of our cooks! The Shoe Pac was a military version of the typical Bean snow boot with leather tops and rubber bottoms and insulation. It was supposed to have been reserved for the front line troops, and some rather frank statements were made in the company kitchen tent. We bitched and bellyached about what we had seen all the way back to the battalion, and, eventually, every man was issued a pair before the end of January. Though easier to walk in than the buckle arctics, we later found that they had a tendency to overheat the feet which had an uncomfortable effect after exertion when the temperature fell below zero Fahrenheit as it did many nights during January.

As January wore on, our first copies of <u>Stars and Stripes</u> and word of mouth reports informed us of the gradual Allied advance on the other sectors of the Bulge. It was obvious that our turn to join this offensive would come sooner or later. We had been lucky, for the infantry fighting forward through the snows of the coldest European winter in fifty years had no shelter for the night, and minor wounds often meant frozen death from shock. Oil froze in the engine blocks of vehicles, and tanks found it difficult to maintain traction on the icy roads. One day, during the third week in January, we were ordered to test fire all our weapons. We were issued leather mittens with openings in the palm for the gloved trigger fingers, and patrol activity increased. By now rumors of our coming offensive commitment were constant.

My selection for a patrol came at dusk of what promised to be a very cold night in mid-January. It was our platoon's turn, and Sgt. Degamo was making up a twelve man patrol from each of the three squads; the mission to capture one or more German prisoners for interrogation. Degamo said I would be the point man with my BAR since they needed as much fire power as possible up front in case of trouble. I protested that I was night blind, might lead them into a trap, etc., holding up my glasses for him to observe the thickness of the lenses. My foxhole buddy, Jim Speer, confirmed that I was blind as a bat at night, and it was later decided that I would take up the rear as the get-away man to provide fire cover while returning. The patrol leader was an unusual fellow from another squad named Ray Flick who had come in as a replacement. He was unique in actually showing enthusiasm for our violent way of life. Flick volunteered for patrols, and there was a rumor that he had ridden shotgun for a mob boss back home in Detroit. (He was actually from southwestern Pennsylvania.) Stocky, of indeterminate age with pale blond hair and expressionless grey eyes, he was not very impressive looking, but his actions belied his appearance. In short order, he had armed himself with a Thompson submachine gun acquired somehow, possibly taken at gunpoint from a tanker. They were not issued in the rifle companies.

Thus armed, Flick led us into the night towards the German lines. Most of us had been given bedsheets

49

to use for camouflage. Our helmets were covered with strips of white sheet. I wore my Christmas scarf and wool knit cap below the helmet liner. I had left my wallet and personal effects with Jim. It was silently understood what his responsibility was in regard to them. It was so cold, the snow crunched loudly under our boots. Fortunately, there was no moon, and the wind was blowing, which tended to mask the sound. Past our last observation post manned by two GIs with a sound powered phone, we ascended the steep ridge that marked no man's land, the enemy positions somewhere on the other side. At the top of the ridge, the word was passed that the German lines were just beyond a sunken road lined with trees at the base of the ridge. We trudged through the deep snow to the sunken lane and took up positions - a party of four at each end of the lane facing in all directions and a party of three with Flick to try to find a prisoner on the east side of the lane. During an earlier thaw, the snow had melted on the trees and bushes of the hedgerows on either side of the lane, and the ice rattled in the wind helping to conceal our approach and whispered commands. The minutes dragged on as we peered into the darkness, imaginary figures materializing from the hedgerow as our eyes strained to distinguish objects. The only sound was the clicking of the ice chandeliers.

Suddenly, I sensed that I was all alone. Looking around, I saw two of the other men who had been with me turning the corner of the hedgerow and heading up the hill. Get-away man indeed! Somebody hadn't passed the word. Voices sounded from the German positions nearby and then a burp gun (Schmeisser machine pistol) opened up - br-r-rip, br-r-rip, followed by the heavier pounding of a machine gun. It was time to go. As I struggled up the hill it seemed like a slow motion dream. I wanted to run, but it was impossible with the weight of the weapon, the depth of the snow, and the steepness of the climb. Retreating figures were far above me. Bullets were hitting the hedgerow, and then flares popped overhead. In training, we were always told to freeze in position when this happened since the slightest movement of the shadow cast by your figure disclosed your presence. I froze with one arm outstretched and tried to remain motionless waiting for the machine gunner to begin traversing up the hill. The men above me had done the same. The flares died and the flight went on. I caught up back at the OP soaking wet from the exertion. Flick had captured a very frightened seventeen year old Panzer Grenadier with all his identification papers and Division insignia. We had gotten rid of ours when we first went into combat. Walking up behind a hedgerow he had literally yanked him backwards through it and grabbed his mouth before he had a chance to sound the alarm, a feat that would have been impossible without the wind. By the time we reached our lines my sweaty woolen shirt had already begun to freeze. Congratulations were passed up from Captain Bill Smith himself, and Flick's legend was confirmed.

Several large and heavily armed combat patrols probed at the enemy lines on subsequent nights. Extra rations of ammunition were issued along with small blocks of TNT with fuses attached for blasting holes in the frozen ground - the tell tale sign that we were about to go on the offensive. We heard of a case of a suspicious gunshot wound in the foot of one of the new replacements. A man in our squad claimed he had stepped on his glasses by mistake and had to be sent back to Division for a new pair. He and we all knew he had gauged his timing carefully - he would miss the attack. No one spoke to him. We sorted out our belongings. I determined that the picture and leather frame would go with me, but that the book on upland game shooting would have to remain in this Godforsaken pasture field along with other odds and ends.

Late in the afternoon, after distribution of the explosive blocks, we were taken up to an observation point and shown the direction of our attack. There would be no artillery fire to cover us; Col. Scott had planned a "surprise attack", though the 2nd and 9th Divisions on our right and left, respectively, would be attacking with heavy artillery preparation. I began to question the wisdom of this plan, in view of the lack of cover and the width of the valley we were to cross. Another problem with the attack plan was that it was to be a night of an almost full moon. The snow was deep and there were only enough white bedsheets for one lead man in each squad. We would stand out like black bulls-eyes on a white background, I said. Kelly lost his temper and told me to find myself another squad and platoon. I was nothing but a smart-ass college kid, etc. The tension must have been eating away at him because he got more furious as he chewed me out. I was appalled, for he really wanted to transfer me to a strange platoon shorn of the only status I had acquired in eighteen months of service: BAR man and acting non-com - to become a rifleman among relative strangers, an internal exile shunned as a pariah. At first, I shouted back just as angrily, but moderated to an almost pleading tone when I realized the depth of his rage. Finally mollified, Kelly dropped the subject. I felt hollow, physically ill, as if I had skirted the abyss of a danger as great as the approaching attack.

A special dinner was sent up from the rear after dark - steak a la Ardennes, dairy cow with mashed potatoes and cake - another foreboding sign. By candlelight, Speer and I took turns making up our bedrolls and sorting through our household effects one last time. I stripped the BAR down into its component parts and oiled them all. I could actually do this with my eyes closed, including the removal of the ejector and firing pin, and I made sure that every moving part was wiped clean and then lubricated.

The word came to move out at 3:00 a.m. and we filed down into the moonlit plain, hugging traces of hedgerow lines and shattered trees wherever we could. The temperature seemed to have dropped very sharply. I can remember our company commander, "Smitty", standing on a slight rise chewing gum beside his radio man and the 1st Sgt., Ed Orlando. The radio man was blowing gently into his mouthpiece, trying to raise the battalion. Even if we didn't have any affection for the C.O., he was the right man for the job. No clumsy overcoat for him; just a field jacket and muffler, pants bloused smartly over his shoepacs, carbine on his shoulder. Nothing ever seemed to perturb him. The snow had drifted and was several feet deep in places. The slow trek across the valley seemed interminable. It seemed to me that our squad was the point of the regimental attack, the lead squad of the lead platoon of the lead company of the lead battalion in the attack plan. We moved past the company CP group and the other platoons into our position of honor. The edge of the forest loomed up pitch black. A distant thundering on our right and left indicated that the 2nd and 9th Divisions were moving out with their artillery firing behind them. All was silent behind us. We reached a final hedgerow

53

in front of the woods beyond which were four or five tall pines on a slight rise about fifty yards from our objective. There seemed to be a communication trench on the other side of the hedgerow. Lt. Herring said that our squad would move out to the pine trees and provide protective fire while the rest of the company swept into the woods on our right. Typically, he led the way for us. At this point, it is more natural for me to shift back into the present tense, since what occurred remains forever frozen in my mind as if it had a special time dimension of its own, akin to the death sequence in Ambrose Bierce's Civil War story, "An Occurrence at Owl Creek Bridge".

We slip through the hedgerow and run for the rise, throwing ourselves to the ground by the pines. A rifle grenade is fired at the woods and several M-I's begin firing. Jim Speer runs past me toward the communication trench. I cock the BAR and pull the trigger; the bolt slides forward; but nothing happens. I repeat the process over and over, but the gun does not fire - the firing pin has apparently frozen in the intense cold. Immediately, answering heavy machine gun fire twinkles at positions inside the forest. John Herring runs over to see what my problem is; helps untangle the bedroll rope that has become entangled on my entrenching tool and then runs back to give encouragement to the men at the other end of the squad. Gillen and Gutsweiler, who had been designated my ammunition bearers, are to my left. They seem to have sunk down in the snow. I call to them - there is no reply. A new machine gun fires - it seems to be within twenty yards of us - the sound is deafening - the pieces of bark are flying from the pine trees beside us. Only one BAR opens up on our side with distinctive bursts of two and three rounds each and then falls silent. None of our machine guns fires. Others must be having weapon malfunctions. Suddenly, red flashes burst in the snow around us as mortar shells rain down. A shock wave hits me without sensation of sound, and it feels as if a giant has kicked me in the left thigh with football cleats. Something warm is trickling into my pants. Every man in the squad seemed to be a lifeless form except me. The mortaring and machine gun fire continues till daybreak and then subsides temporarily.

One of the motionless forms beside me suddenly comes to life and crawls over to me. It is Badell, a Jewish boy from Brooklyn. He says that Lt. Herring and the other ten men in the squad are dead. We would have to get ready for the inevitable German counter-attack. He offers me a rifle and a bandoleer of eight-round magazines. I think he is insane. The company attack had never been launched and without my automatic weapon functioning, the odds are overwhelming. Badell raises himself on his elbows and aims towards the communication ditch in front of us. A burst of machine gun fire tears through his right forearm and biceps. Another bullet creases the right side of his face, the blood streaming down. "Try to get to the rear", I whisper, and pull the bandoleers over his head, as if they would do me some good. He starts to crawl away without having uttered a word of complaint, after wishing me luck. He almost reaches the hedgerow when another burst of fire rings out. It is unlikely that he ever made it.

I lie among the silent figures of the squad. They look as if they are sleeping. Only a few stains of blood show on their uniforms. The cold is so intense that it seems to have stopped the bleeding in my leg, but everything begins to feel numb. I try to crawl sideways an inch at a time, but every time I make three or four small snail slow movements with my arms or legs, the nearby gunner fires a burst, pine splinters striking me about the face. The tree seems to be shredding at the level of my head. I assume the position of my dead companions. Time has no meaning. It could have been an hour or only minutes later that American 105 mm shells come warbling in to explode on the German positions right in front of us, shell fragments whizzing overhead. At last, someone has come to their senses at regiment. I feel sure that I will die there and determine to make a run for it with the next incoming salvo to hold down the opposing machine gunners heads. Here they come - some more on the way - perfect targeting! I leap to my feet and take two strides for the hedgerow, but the left leg collapses. I've disclosed my position and crawl as fast as my hands, elbows and right knee will move me. I get through the hedgerow as shells still burst behind, and lie exhausted for a moment.

Bodies lie all around. It looks like most of the platoon. Counseller, our company jeep driver, who had been pressed into front line service, is lying on his back. A big man, over two hundred pounds, he is staring fixedly at the greying sky. He says that he cannot move. I try to get him to roll over on top of me; so that I can carry him back, but he says it is impossible. I tell him I will try to get someone to help him, and crawl towards the rear. A short distance away a large hole appears. I tumble in among three other men from another platoon. One of them has a walkie-talkie. I stand up to point out the German machine gun positions, but they pull me down, saying there are snipers on platforms in the trees. I finally persuade them to let me try to direct a fire order for our 60 mm mortars and talk in some rounds upon the German positions that I hold responsible for the destruction of our platoon. I tell them about Counseller.

They say they will try to help him. I am advised to leave to get treatment after one man straps an aid pack on my leg, indicating by his voice that the wound is quite large. He is sure there will be a counter-attack by nightfall. The sky is now grey. More snow is on the way.

The leg feels so numb that I am convinced, and they help push me over the edge to crawl through the hedgerow and flop into a shallow communication trench on the other side. I have lost my helmet and find it hard to see as snow fogs my glasses, and the wool knit cap falls over one eye. An occasional shot rings out, and American machine guns are now hammering to the left of our platoon's position. It must be hundreds of yards back along the trench before instinct tells me I should be near the center of the company and as far away from the woods as the trench will take me. I crawl out; work through the hedgerow and find a line of men pinned down by sniper fire. One who looks and talks like a new replacement offers to help me get up, pulling me to my feet. A shot rings out and he yells, a bullet through his leg; "I'm shot, I'm shot." "Of course you're shot, you silly son of a bitch," I mutter. I can only feel anger at his heroics. We're lucky not to be dead. Now the two of us continue the long crawl back to where somebody says the company aid station is located - another hundred yards.

The medics are at work behind a slight ridge. Their morphine syrettes have frozen and they are thawing them in their armpits. My bandage is changed and tightened, as I have started to bleed again. The needle goes in; a blanket thrown over me, and then a blissful sensation of warmth steals through my body. It is now nightfall, and snow is hissing down. The medic checks us every hour with a gentle kick to keep us awake and responding to his inquiries. The needle goes in again and I drift off to sleep. The snow must be an inch deep on the blanket when I feel a litter being placed under me for a long carry to the base of the hill to be strapped on the front of a weasel. "Thanks you guys, thanks a lot," I say, overcome with gratitude. We churn back on the tracked vehicle through the snow to a regimental aid station. Our battalion has sustained casualties of approximately thirty percent. Twenty-seven of the thirty-six in our platoon are casualties, and ten of the twelve in the squad are dead. Someone pours brandy down our throats, and one feels like part of a happy family scene; talking, calling out for news of our buddies, feeling a tremendous weight of fear slide away. Most of us are going to live.

An ambulance took a load of us to a hospital in Verviers, where a ward was crammed with Company G men on canvas cots. Pain racked my stomach wall and thighs. I finally realized that the muscles had frozen and were thawing out. I was taken into the operating room to have the wound cleaned out and the flesh trimmed. Downey, my red-haired competitor for the girl in Commerce, Texas during an all too brief two day pass, lay moaning on his cot. He had lost several fingers on one hand. "My hand, my hand - what'll I do," he cried. Others were hurt far worse, but we were disturbed by the psychic effect of Downey's complaints. Moreover, he was spoiling our enjoyment of the miracle that had brought us this far from the front. Somebody yelled at him to shut up, and he fell silent for a time. Figge, the platoon scout, was there with bullet wounds. He claimed to have shot two Germans running for the communication trench with his grease gun. He was considered reliable, and this was accepted as fact. The talk flowed back and forth. It was a high school reunion - friends seen or heard from that were presumed dead. There was a heart-warming rumor that Colonel Scott had been relieved of his command and put in charge of a PX chain in Paris.

I noticed that I flinched involuntarily at every odd sound, particularly the sibilant noise of whispering voices or the rustle of paper. The others had the same reflexes. We had become as wary as foxes, our ganglia tuned to a level of consciousness not normally experienced by civilized man. Time still hadn't begun to move in its normal sequence. An hour or a day after my first trip to the operating room, I was on a hospital train, box cars with stretcher racks three high. The train was fully loaded. We were going to Paris - ah, what bliss, I always had a romantic attachment to trains, and here we were headed for Paris!

Upon arrival we were taken through rainy streets to a hospital evacuated by the Germans only a few months before. The ward was filled with representatives from the divisions in the big offensive; 78th, 9th, 99th, 2nd, the Big Red One, and the 82nd Airborne. How nice that they kept us all together to share our experiences. I still flinched at odd noises, but my mind was now telling me to relax; it's only the man in the next bed turning the pages of a tattered magazine. A very frail, pale blond nurse, who seemed too young for her occupation, sat me up in bed to catcalls from adjacent beds: "Now be a good boy and take your bath." She shampooed my hair and washed my face and ears. The wash basin turned coal black, was emptied and refilled; next swollen hands and feet, and finally she trimmed my gruesome toenails. She remains the image of a sweet sister of Charity drying the dripping feet of another survivor of a holocaust. It was early February, and my third brief contact with soap and water since we left camp D-6 at the end of October.

The time came for another trip to the operating room: bright lights and a big needle. It was sodium pentothal. They were going to probe for more shell fragments. "Count to ten", the doctor said. I made it to four and drifted with increasing speed into unconsciousness. I awakened back in the ward to a radio playing Glenn Miller. Chow had been served and a tray was on my bed. I sat up, took a mouthful, and then fell backwards asleep on the pillow amid the sound of laughter in the ward.

Near the front line - early November, 1944

CP on Elsenborn Ridge

The "groundhog" look

The coldest winter in Europe in fifty years

Evacuation of dead or wounded

CHAPTER 6

After a week or so, some of us were moved from Paris to a tent hospital on the Cherbourg Peninsula near the town of La Haye du Puits. Each ward was in a huge tent holding perhaps forty men. They were equipped with coal burning iron stoves on which we toasted bread with twisted coat hangers. In addition to two thirtyish nurses and enlisted orderlies, we had a young German PW from Stuttgart, who helped serve our meals. The ward was integrated. We had a black Red Ball express truck driver who had one leg terribly burned from flaming gasoline in a wreck. His skin grafts just didn't seem to take, though he cheerfully joined our endless poker games.

I had obtained an Army issue German phrase book that I thumbed constantly seeking a superficial proficiency in the language suited to coming events: "Kommen sie heraus, waffen niederlegen, hande hoch", etc. This led me into frequent attempts at conversation with the German orderly. Though he seemed likable enough, I couldn't refrain from remarks about Hitler and the coming Gotterdamerung that finally led the senior American orderly to ask me to knock it off; I was disturbing the work routine.

I made the acquaintance of Ted Rice, a twenty-six year old platoon sergeant from the 82nd Airborne who had jumped at Sicily, Normandy and Nijmegen, and had been wounded each time. A graduate of Taft School, he had worked on Wall Street before enlisting. After the stitches were removed from my leg, we teamed up for a self-designed physical therapy program; hiking and jogging through the Norman countryside in pajamas and

66

combat boots. Trading packs of cigarettes with the farmers, we often returned to the ward with bottles of the local Calvados, raw and very potent, to enliven the evening routine.

Somebody had found a large map of central Europe, and I posted it on a bulletin board hanging from one of the tent poles. AFN Luxembourg continued to broadcast news of the Allied advances interspersed with Glenn Miller, Dorsey, Artie Shaw, and Count Basie. Roosevelt, Churchill, and Stalin had already met at Yalta. Montgomery was making massive preparations for the crossing of the Rhine at Wesel. The American 9th Army had crossed the Roer and with Divisions of the 1st Army were closing up to the Rhine near Cologne. Though we didn't know it by the end of February, the 99th had teamed up with 3rd Armored Division for lightning advances across the Cologne plain, and was the first American division to reach the Rhine. Then, on the 7th of March, a combat command of the 9th Armored took the bridge at Remagen, and the 99th, hurriedly shifted south, was the first full division across into the bridgehead. Then Patton upstaged Monty too by getting a crossing at Oppenheim, and the end appeared in sight.

One day in March, our orderlies went on pass to the fishing port of Granville and returned that night wide-eyed with tales of narrow escapes from a German commando attack launched from the Channel Islands. Perhaps driven by exhortations from the Fuhrer bunker, two E boats had swept into the port and unloaded assault teams who shot up things, and blew up a locomotive on a siding. The infantry men in the ward roared with laughter and demanded endless details of their harrowing experiences.

Rice was determined to join the 82nd, and I felt compelled to get back to my unit, not only because it was something I really belonged to, but because of a slowly developing survivor's guilt complex that made me fixated to be with the company for another combat engagement before the end of the war in Europe. The objective was to return before it was all over, but not too soon. If we had to go to the Pacific, we wanted to go with our own units. After a month of our daily workouts, Rice and I were given permission to bypass the organized physical therapy classes that lasted for thirty days, and to move into the replacement depot system for return to our units.

Rice and I took a train to Paris, but were shortly separated as my orders took me to a replacement depot in the dingy town of Etampes near Paris. After a few days there, a great number of us from various "repple depples" were loaded in boxcars for a train ride up the Meuse Valley to Liege where we loaded again in open tractor trailer cattle trucks of the Transportation Corps for a ride to the industrial town of Stolberg near the ruins of Aachen where we bedded down in an abandoned factory. A brewery nearby provided an ample supply of dark beer that we hauled out in five gallon jernicans.

Stolberg was relatively undamaged, and I passed the time walking the hilly streets and practicing my German with a few of the frauleins, one of whom surprisingly invited me to a modest dinner with her family of ten friendly Rhinelanders. They seemed honest and open. There was no attempt to hide the fact that the fifteen year old son had been in the Hitler Youth. As the father explained, it was almost like the Boy Scouts. Despite some mental reservations about this explanation, I felt relaxed and at home. It was a useful corrective to the hatred of Germans that had begun to form in the last month of combat.

In a few days, a group of us representing members of the Division returning from hospitals and new replacements were issued M-1 rifles and a basic load of ammunition and left Stolberg in two and a half ton trucks to find the 99th Division. We crossed the Rhine on a temporary bridge well downstream from Remagen and passed through riotous scenes in the "liberated" towns of the Ruhr pocket. Thousands of French, Belgian, Polish slave laborers and Russian PW's lined the streets to shout and wave as we roared through. Inevitably, it seemed the Russians and the Americans were swept by a great feeling of special comradeship: "Russki, Russki - Americanski, Tovarisch" was shouted back and forth. Of all the nationalities, they seemed the most simpatico in their openness and lack of sophistication. No one who experienced those days in Germany can ever forget the mood of a swiftly approaching apocalyptic peace with a reality of its own equal to the tragedy of the coming Cold War.

We caught up with the Division rear somewhere in the Ruhr pocket and veterans and green replacements alike, attended orientation sessions on the history of the unit and the type of combat ahead of us. From the briefing given by a captain, it was clear that we had returned to a new outfit, experienced and aggressive: infantry support for the 3rd Armored on the Cologne Plain, Remagen, the critical break-out across the Wied River and the drive into the Ruhr pocket against occasional German armored units and deadly flak batteries. The casualties had been equal to those in the Bulge. After two nights in a village in the foothills of the Hartz mountains, several hundred of us loaded up in

69

trucks and caught up with our assigned companies near Bamberg as the Division was transferred to the 3rd Army for the final drive on the Alpine Redoubt that diehard SS units were supposed to form in southern Bavaria and Austria. We were to make an assault crossing of the Danube River.

Mortar barrage in the Remagen bridgehead
March, 1945

THE ROAD TO EINING

CHAPTER 7

In the summer of 1988, Harriet and I signed on for a battlefield tour called "D-Day to the Rhine" led by the late Charles MacDonald, military historian and former company commander in the 2nd Division. We left the tour at Wiesbaden and took the Vienna train from Mainz to Regensburg on the Danube where we got our cheap Europa rental car. On the map, Eining, where we had made our assault crossing, looked about twenty miles away. By some miracle, I had correctly interpreted the directions given in German by the rental lady, and headed in the right direction on the highway towards Kelheim, where we turned off on a secondary road and followed the upstream course of the Danube.

After one wrong turn, I was sure we were there: the high, pine crested ridge on the left, the swift-running river on the right, its banks shielded by alders, the steeple of the church surrounded by the tile covered roofs of the town's buildings straight ahead. What was different was the appearance of the fields leading to the town; no longer unfenced pasture strewn with dandelions, but dense with maize. It was clear as we approached that some buildings had been added. The old couple's house where I made our headquarters, and used their fenced yard as a prisoner of war enclosure, was nowhere in sight. In its place was a large structure, either a school house or an apartment building. The picket fence on the left of the roadway where I had rested my M-1, no longer afforded a clear shot at the church steeple. There was a new house in the way. But in its essential character, Eining had not changed. It was still a farm town, evidenced by the

72

mooing from the barns attached to the houses and the passage of modern diesel tractors on the streets bringing in ensilage for feed. In the middle of the town, on the left, was a large courtyard with houses on two sides, and a barrack-like barn on the third side through which a farmer was driving his tractor. That must have been where we first lined the prisoners up to check them for pistols and knives, and to obtain our souvenirs. The barn must have been where the debate had raged over the disposition of the mortally wounded SS man. Across the street, an "elderly" man in his late sixties or early seventies, was cleaning windows. "Waren sie hier in funf und fierzig?" "Nein, man da droben war" was the response, as he pointed to the next house where a pleasant looking woman of about forty was watering her geraniums on a second floor balcony. I started a mental rehearsal of my question, and then realized the futility of it, for she probably hadn't been born then. The time lapse formed a formidable barrier.

The car rental procedure had taken too long, and it was already late afternoon with the hotel in Munich sixty miles away. Obviously, there wasn't going to be any time for house-to-house interviewing, and I felt a little hesitant anyhow. Maybe we would find someone who had lost a family member to our grenades, machine gun and rifle fire. Harriet and I walked up to a newly stuccoed church and took more pictures. I worried about the ASA setting because I wanted to send a set of good ones to Ray Flick. We went back to the car, and headed south for Abendsberg where the SS men had been shot down when they tried to surrender after machine gunning the lead elements of the company from windows from which white bed sheets of surrender had been draped. The Eining that I had been looking for, and not really

73

found, was already dwindling in the rear view mirror. The only way to get there was through a sustained effort at recollection.

I had caught up with the Division at Bamberg, north of Nurenburg, after the conclusion of the Ruhr Pocket Campaign. My sojourn in the field hospital at La Haye du Puits on the Cherbourg peninsula and in the replacement depots, had saved me from the drive with the 3rd Armored on the Cologne plain, the Remagen bridge head and exposure to the flak guns of the Ruhr, though I had not been malingering. When I found the company there were only a few that I knew. Ray Flick had my squad, and I was made his assistant. Sutphen was acting platoon leader, and Nelson was acting platoon sergeant of the second platoon. Lt. Greenough had returned as company executive officer, and we had a new CO, Capt. Bill Smith having been wounded in the Ruhr Pocket. Other than the indomitable men of the weapons platoon, it seemed like almost everyone else was a replacement.

There were a lot of other changes, too. The day after my return, we were assembled in a school room and given a chalk talk on the blackboard by Lt. Greenough and the platoon leaders. Our next assignment was to make a surprise assault crossing of the Danube near a little town to create a bridgehead for the 14th Armored Division which would drive for the Austrian border. The town was reported to be defended by elements of a Scandinavian SS unit called the Viking Division that had fought in Russia. The blackboard diagram made by Lt. Greenough stressed the position of the three rifle platoons: one down the main street using fire and movement from building to building; one to sweep the south bank of the river; and the other to go south of the town to cover that flank. An additional element of the attack plan would come from our recently acquired fourth rifle platoon of black volunteers from port and quarter-master battalions commanded by a black platoon sergeant named Henry. They would form deep flank coverage by going up a steep ridge to the southeast of the town.

In addition to the uniqueness of having such an academic preparation for coming events, we had an opportunity to practice with our means of transport across the river by launching and paddling assault boats over a nearby waterway considerably smaller and less swift than the Danube. An added bonus was given in the form of tanks to ride all the way down to save our energies for the assault crossing. We rode the tanks all one day and part of the following night, bedding down in some woods near the juncture of the Altmuhl Canal and the Danube. At dawn, we moved down through another wooded area to the river's edge screened from the other shore, and met some of the Division engineers who had brought the boats down to the river. Every man was issued a paddle, and the engineers held the boats at the water's edge as we climbed in. The opposite shore was also screened by a dense grove of alder-like trees around a swampy area; a good selection all around.

However, once cast off, our boat holding a dozen men was soon spinning like a top in the surging current, all attempts at unified strokes lost to the excitement of the moment and the current's strength. Somehow we made the far shore, and not a shot had been fired to disturb the peace of the late April morning. As we emerged from the swampy area and spread out in our attack formation, the climate rapidly changed as machine gun fire both from the high ridge to the south of the road into town, and from the buildings to the west in front of us swept overhead. Mortar shells began to fall near the shore, but their explosions were muffled by mud of the impact area. As we hit the dirt and lay down as flat as possible among the dandelions, I started to fall asleep, incredible as it may seem, fatigued by the change in routine from hospital ward and replacement depots. Probably only sixty seconds passed when I awoke to a shouted command being sent back: "Sutphen up front." Cursing a blue streak, our acting platoon leader from West Virginia ran crouching forward followed by two heavy machine gun crews from H Company, who set up their water-cooled weapons in open view of the town and began sending a cascade of .30 caliber fire that caused the slate of the tiled roofs to jettison upward in a black cloud that hovered there as long as the guns fired. Suddenly, everyone rose up the moment that the last belt was fired and began running forward, screaming strange cries that may have been similar to rebel yells, another new element that had been absent from winter warfare or even our training in Texas. Four middle aged prisoners, either Volksturm or German railway employees impressed into the town's defense, were being herded forward at gun point ahead of the leading element. One was being forced to carry the company SCR300 radio on his back, a little balding man stumbling along with the antenna whipping back and forth to his clumsy movements, clearly a violation of the Geneva Convention. By the side of the road, the platoon medic, a tall, quiet replacement, sat on a bank calmly observing the battle with his helmet off waiting to be called into service.

Our platoon, the 2nd, was to go through the middle of town, and I thought Flick said that our squad was to go to the left of the main street to provide flank protection for the squads storming ahead on the main route. I ran across the roadway to a picket fence on the left-hand side, and realized that it was not an easy obstacle to overcome. Silent house windows stared ahead, and above them loomed the steeple of the church at the far end of town with a clearly visible aperture from which a weapon could be fired. After resting the M-1 on the fence, I fired two full eight-round clips at the opening in the steeple, then climbed over and fell to the ground. A torrent of fire and grenade explosions was moving down the main street, but my section of town was very quiet. I suddenly realized I was all alone. Better to move forward to the shelter of building walls than go back over the picket fence. I moved forward with rifle at the ready, and then thrust it quickly into aiming position as a man's head bobbed up from a foxhole in the ground, and then down again. Three times or more this movement was repeated, and it slowly became clear that the town idiot was the only occupant. I sent him grinning to the rear, glad that I hadn't opened fire, and moved towards a barn on my right with a large opening for wagons beyond which there seemed to be a courtyard.

At the courtyard, I crouched by the edge of a wall to survey the situation. Firing seemed to have almost stopped except for an occasional round. The sound of hob-nail boots coming towards me on the main street was surprising until Flick and other men of the squad appeared with a large contingent of prisoners with a half dozen of their backbone, men of the Viking SS, obvious by their smarter uniforms and lightning flashes on their collars. Using my phrase book German, I told them to keep their hands up behind their heads, to line up and to surrender all weapons including knives: "Hande hoch, antreten sie; waffen niederlegen; haben sie messer bei sich?" They obeyed readily forming into four or five files. A few knives clattered on the cobble stones.

A report came in from the right flank platoon. One man had a narrow escape when a panzerfaust blew in a hen house where he was looking for eggs. A sixteen year old boy had been shot by the SS for refusing to defend the town. A slim, blondish SS man at the end of the file next to me attracted Flick's attention because of his overly military bearing. He spoke a little English; said he was Danish and had been forced to join the SS, etc. Flick's jaw muscles began to tighten, and he suddenly hit him under the chin with a vicious uppercut, sending the Dane to the cobble stones spitting out teeth and blood, causing a visible movement among the rest of the prisoners. Flick's rage may also have been caused by the irony of having Danes and Norwegians appearing as the enemy when we assumed all of their fellow countrymen were on our side.

By now, all firing in the town had stopped except for the crack of an occasional shot that seemed to come from a house several buildings away on the main street to the east of the courtyard. I entered the house next to me, and carefully ascended the stairs poking my rifle through an open door into a bedroom facing to the east. Keeping back from the windows, I searched in vain for signs of movement behind windows in houses across the street that would reveal the presence of the hidden sniper. A scurry of movement sounded down below as Flick emerged on the street with a borrowed BAR using the Danish SS man as a human shield running towards the second house across the street, another violation of the Geneva Convention. He had spotted something. He fired burst after burst at a second floor window, and entered the doorway with his prisoner ahead of him. More bursts of fire: two round sequences and then steady automatic until the firing finally stopped. He emerged with a new prisoner, a steadily widening dark spot on his civilian jacket marking a wound. Flick had a bullet wound through the side of his neck. When he returned with them to the courtyard, we stared at the new prisoner. He was about thirty-five, entirely clad in civilian clothes except for jack boots. He must have gone insane from too many years of Nazi ideology. The other prisoners, now allowed to sit, moved away from him as he slumped to the cobble stones. I spotted a German medic by his arm band, and repeatedly had to order him at gun point to dress the man's wound.

All of the prisoners were eventually led away to another location, and the platoon assembled in the barn where another SS man that I hadn't seen before lay on the ground, arms flung out, obviously dying. In a low whisper, he begged for a drink of water and a debate ensued; give him a bit of surcease or not? Nelson and Sutphen said no - to hell with the son of a bitch. Others said yes, he's had it. The platoon medic won the debate without a word. He held a canteen to the lips of the mortally wounded enemy, and the argument stopped.

Flick was smiling in spite of the blood from his neck wound. He told me that the squad of replacements was mine. He had his pass to the rear, and was through for the duration. He walked out to find the aid station as we told him goodbye. He had earned a rest. I thought about the days ahead. We were to set up a perimeter defense for the night, and then move out in the morning on foot towards a town called Abendsberg. I was exhausted in spite of the hiking and jogging Rice and I had done on the Cherbourg peninsula. I discussed the matter with Sutphen, who said that he would leave me behind with three men, all new replacements culled from each rifle platoon, to guard the prisoners until the treadway bridge for the armored division had been completed near the east side of town which was named Eining. We took up positions in houses on the outskirts with half of the men on outpost duty while others slept. Before dark, I climbed up to the top of the church steeple out of curiosity, and found an MG42 with a full belt of ammunition lying on the floor. I was pleased with the discovery. Maybe a few lucky shots had panicked the occupants into a hurried departure, and I had contributed something towards the company's success.

All in all, the company had been lucky. Elements of the 395th Regt. had suffered heavy casualties trying to cross further upstream. They were opposed by men of the SS Nibelungen Division, which had been hastily formed the previous month out of raw recruits and the instructors and cadets at the SS officer candidate school at Bad Tolz. It was about midnight on my tour of guard duty when I heard a sound moving on the river road coming from the west towards my position at the western end of town. It was an elderly man with a bicycle coming back to his home. I chaperoned him down the main street so that he wouldn't be shot for failure to know the password and then turned in for the night. It had been a long day.

In the morning, the company formed up with the rest of the regiment that marched through town for the advance on Abendsberg and the Isar River. With the other members of my four men guard detachment, I moved back to the company aid station on the eastern fringe of the town, the home of an aged couple, in whose fenced yard there were now over one hundred prisoners of war, the smell of unwashed bodies coming from the damp wool of their field grey and Turkish tobacco creating an aroma distinctly German that seemed to blend appropriately with the odor of manure that permeated Eining. The other three men of my detail were eighteen year old privates who had come into the company somewhere between Remagen and the Ruhr pocket. Though I was only a PFC, I was now a squad leader, and my year in the company established my authority over the guard detail. We set up guard around the picket fence announcing in loud tones, with appropriate gestures and a few German phrases, that we would throw hand grenades into the lot if anybody tried to escape. Food and water for them was not our concern, though we let the elderly couple give them a few loaves of bread and some water from the well. It was raw and cold, and we did not interfere with their taking sticks of kindling from the owner's supply to build small fires.

We cleared out the living room where plasma bottles were hanging from lamps. A bloody pack contained a volume of Oxford verse, probably belonging to a former ASTP man. There were two other inhabitants, two women evacuees from Berlin, a doctor's wife and a younger woman with a baby. The doctor's wife appeared to be in her late thirties. Her slightly olive complexion, dark hair, and sharp features suggested southern European ancestry. Well educated, she spoke good, though heavily accented English. The other woman was much younger, a pretty blond, though rather chubby. She spoke no English and appeared to be of a quite different social class from the doctor's wife. God knows what had happened to their homes and husbands.

After the first night, the treadway bridge still had not been completed. The sniper prisoner was still bleeding from his wound; so I went down to the river and talked with men on an amphibious Dukw. A medical jeep appeared a few hours later, and our most fanatical captive was driven away. The next day, the bridge was completed, and as the armored column formed up, I led the prisoners down to cross on the walkway over the pontoon boats beside the vehicle tracks. Despite or, perhaps, misunderstanding my exhortation, "Nicht Ein, Zwei, Drei" they were soon marching in Teutonic unison causing the walkway to heave and fall in an alarming fashion. I breathed a sigh of relief on the other side as I turned them over to the first MP that I saw.

Back at the house, I was shaken by one of my detail telling me that five or six of our own dead were still in and about the town. One, now frozen in rigor mortis, his features a mottled yellow color, lay a block away close to the house the sniper had used. I flagged down a command car passing through; explained the situation and asked the occupants to contact Regiment somewhere to the south. Many hours later, a two and a half ton truck came back from Regiment, and we proceeded to form a removal detail with the aid of several Polish DPs. Two of Sgt. Henry's black platoon were stretched out on the slope of the high ridge below a silent MG42. Another man was slumped in a foxhole near the position of the platoon medic who had sat in the open so nonchalantly during the assault. I could not bring myself to go into the foxhole. One of the new replacements who spoke with a hillbilly twang jumped in and lifted the body out by main force. We carried it to the truck where we placed it as gently as possible under the circumstances. We loaded six bodies altogether. The town's people must have removed their own dead.

Perhaps we should have gone in the truck with the bodies in the direction of the regiment, but no one had specifically said when or how we were to return. We went back to the old couple's house where the town burgermeister was waiting for an audience with me. He wanted my backing for his plan to redistribute certain scarce items such as flour and sugar among the civilians. I gravely considered and gave my consent, for I was now the ranking representative of the occupying power, clothed with regal authority - a twenty year old private first class.

There seemed to be a general consensus among the inhabitants of the old couple's home that a party was in order. C rations were heated up with eggs. Some homemade wine and schnapps came up from the cellar. A victrola appeared and we danced a clumsy tango or two with the doctor's wife and the young mother amid flickering candle light. Despite the gaiety, everyone stayed on their best behavior, and the two women eventually retired to bed on the second floor while we four GI's bedded down in the first floor living room. Late at night, there was a loud knocking on the door. I had acquired a Belgian automatic and held it ready in one hand as I opened the door, and put my back to the door jamb. A rough American voice asked if we had any booze and women that we could spare. In a rage, I held the muzzle near his head. I told him that we were 393rd Infantry, 99th Division; that the entire town was under our control and to get the hell out, which he did very quickly. The next day, we discussed the situation among ourselves and decided to head in the direction of the regiment before someone questioned our absence. Our rations were almost gone anyhow. The old lady dabbed at her eyes, and the two evacuees gave us kisses to thank us for our temporary protection. We hailed a passing truck, and eventually found our unit well to the south of the Isar River near a town called Vilsbiburg. The company had been briefly in action at Abendsberg and

83

Landshut where the last shots of the war had been fired in our sector. It was almost VE Day. Eining had been the end of the war for me.

Danube crossing - late April, 1945

The inevitable casualties

AFTERMATH

CHAPTER 8

After VE Day, we were reassigned to occupation duty between Wurzburg and Aschaffenburg on the Main River, where I divided my time between refugee screening duty on the nearby autobahn with my future Princeton roommate, Ned Goodnow - looking for likely SS and testing the limits of the non-fraternization edict. Screening refugees was fairly simple. We asked all the adults passing along the autobahn for their Ausweis (identification), but only concentrated our inquiry upon males in the age bracket of twenty to fifty, observing their demeanor. Sometimes the wrong body movements or intonation of voice caused us to detain a suspect for further interrogation at an IPW center. The non-fraternization ban was soon a joke as far as preventing contacts between GIs and German women.

Another interesting assignment was guarding some railroad warehouses in a marshalling yard. One contained thousands of cases of French red bordeaux and vermouth in cases stamped with the Wehrmacht eagle, which soon provided us with liquid refreshment throughout the day, sometimes as early as breakfast in the morning. A more difficult problem was posed by a warehouse filled with cases of canned goulash, which were being pilfered by Polish DPs living nearby. We decided to impose a rationing system of one can per person who arrived on the scene, forbidding removal of cases. The rationing system soon broke down, particularly when our attention was diverted by friendly DPs and their younger women serenading us with Polish songs and toasting the end of the war around a fire.

this, I was given an
ern to the C.O., Captain Bill
ed from a field hospital. I was to
literary skills to write up accounts,
ional, of the heroic exploits of the remaining
s of the company who had been with us from
xas on to try to get them, if not Silver, at least Bronze
stars, which were worth five points in the point system,
which might get us rotated home sooner rather than later.
We never saw any results from my labors, but as I hunted
and pecked away on the company clerk's typewriter, I
realized what a complete sea change had taken place. I
was no longer an ASTP freak, but rather one of the old
men of the company. This was further confirmed when
Smitty asked all of the men who had been at Camp
Maxey to assemble in one of the schoolhouse rooms
where we were billeted to hear him read a draft letter to
Lt. Womack's widow, and to give him any suggested
additions or comments. The schoolhouse was in the town
of Stockstadt, fairly near Aschaffenburg on the other side
of the Main River. Later, we were moved to more rustic
environs up river between Dorfprozelten and
Stadtprozelten. It is to be assumed that this spreading out
of units throughout the German countryside was to
impress the locals with the fact that they had been
completely defeated in the war.

They broke up the Division around the middle of
August. Several thousand of us were put in boxcars for
Le Havre destined to become cadre for a reconstituted
95th Division at Camp Shelby in Mississippi for the
invasion of Japan; so much for staying with the old outfit.
For a time our train was stopped near the French-German
border beside another one decorated with pine boughs
nailed to the outside of the boxcars. The occupants were

Russians, who stared sullenly out a̶ our friendly calls. They had probably b̶ from Wehrmacht labor battalions and were dreading homecoming with good reason.

As the boxcars trundled through the railyard in Amiens, a little French kid was running beside the train hawking newspapers with an enormous black headline: "La Bombe Atomique Est Tombe!" We got as far as Southampton and then to Camp Barton Stacy where we rusticated for two months without unit organization, officers, orders, or pay - no mama, no papa, no Uncle Sam! Somehow, with Red Cross loans, and sale of our prize souvenirs, two men from F Company, John McCoy, Ernie McDaniel, and I managed to get enough funds together to get to London. Ernie picked up a lively cockney lass named Renee Osborne while listening to a soapbox orator at Hyde Park. Renee in turn lined John and me up with two girlfriends who worked at the National City Bank of New York in London for a number of pleasant theater outings. In spite of their east London background, the girls picked all the right shows: Noel Coward, Shakespeare, Marlowe, etc. Later, the three of us managed to travel all the way to Loch Lomond in Scotland in late September - beautiful weather and scenery.

The thing about Renee was if you called the bank to ask your girlfriend for a date, it always seemed that Renee got on the line explaining that your friend had a cold, but she was available to go out. That was alright with me; she was livelier company anyhow, and was a contributing factor to my eventually going AWOL for an entire week.

John McCoy was assigned to guard duty at an abandoned air field near Blackpool, but at the end of

ipped back to Le
to wait for a ship
bacco industry on the
ames of these camps, such
bert Tareyton, and so forth.
n box had contained a mini-pack
rly well distributed through all the
aagine how many millions of cigarettes
to, but it may be too late to bring a class

Sitting in a tent under the rain in November with
nothing to do was enough to drive me out of my mind to
such an extent that I even asked for a job, and for a time
was assigned as an assistant motion picture projector
operator in the camp theater, then later to a troop
movement office where I had access to the forms for
leave status. Life was pretty dull, and it was time for
some adventure, so I forged a pass to London, got a ride
on a motorcycle down to the harbor, found an English
freighter that was going to Gravesend, and hitched a ride,
getting off on the pilot boat when we reached the
Thames. Sure enough, Renee was available for dinner
and a pleasant evening. I later returned to a movement
camp in Southampton. At night, I waited as the roll call
was read for men to board a cross-channel ferry for Le
Havre. Hearing a name that I was familiar with read
twice with no response, I acknowledged my presence the
third time the roll was called, and got back without my
absence being noticed.

My mother's emergency illness at Christmas
eventually brought me home in a C-47 with stops at
Iceland and Gander for refueling. Home seemed
completely disorienting, and it took me a long time to get
readjusted. Driving or walking, I was constantly

surveying familiar terrain for the siting of machine guns or mortars, waking up at the slightest sounds at night, and keeping a loaded .45 nearby. I began to be overwhelmed with a survivor's guilt complex from the events of January 30, 1945. A reunion with McCoy and McDaniel at the McDaniel home in Charleston, West Virginia in September, 1946 was definitely part of the healing process, which had begun when I met Harriet shortly after discharge. I still have the warmest memories of Ernie's family. It all seems like such a long time ago, and yet, in other ways, still so immediate. After all, it was supposed to have been "the best years of our lives."

In May, 1994, Harriet and I joined a mini-reunion with four other former ASTP members and their wives at the home of the McDaniels in West Lafayette, Indiana. John McCoy of Rockford, Illinois had been a BAR man in F Company of our battalion. Trained as a heating engineer under the GI Bill after the war, for the past twenty years he had been selling and maintaining heating systems in China, having married a young Chinese woman from the mainland after the death of his first wife. Ernie was a full professor of psychology at Purdue, having previously been in charge of all educational testing in the state of Kentucky. He had been John's assistant gunner and ammo bearer. Ralph McGinnis from Folsom, Pennsylvania had been a rifleman and platoon scout in my company. With Westinghouse for many years, he had a total of five patents to his credit. Charles McMurray of Webster City, Iowa, never made it overseas, having occurred a serious case of meningitis while at Camp Maxey. He had inherited and greatly expanded a nationally known poultry breeding company in Iowa. Their post war success says a lot about the GI Bill. It also says something about the ASTP.

91

Two friends from F Company:
John McCoy (middle) and Ernest McDaniel (right)

Ernest McDaniel and Renee Osborne
Salisbury Cathedral - September, 1945

Reunion in Charleston, WV - September, 1946

LOOKING BACK

CHAPTER 9

As I vegetated in the movement camp at LeHavre, I thought seriously of re-enlisting and seeking assignment to the Constabulary force that was being formed for occupation duty in the U.S. occupation sector of Germany, but my mother's illness intervened. The bonding to one's unit described earlier in these pages was a pretty general experience in World War II, as evidenced by William Manchester's "Goodbye, Darkness." Beyond that, it is almost impossible to describe what life was like under combat conditions. I am not speaking of the physical hazards and hardships, but rather of the emotional and psychological state that we went through. When I think of Elsenborn Ridge fifty years later, I think mostly of nighttime, bitter cold, and ice crystals sparkling in the exposed dirt of our foxholes. I have lamely described it as like being "on the face of the moon," but it was much more than that. It was as if you were possessed by, and were a part of that landscape. In everyday life, our contact with reality is both extended and quite diluted by the telephone, television, and mail creating a very extended sensory horizon. Under the conditions that I have tried to describe, all reality is compressed into what you can see, hear, and feel. Along with the compression of the external horizon is an elongation of one's sense of time where minutes sometimes seem like hours and days like weeks or months. Perhaps the best analogy would be to the experience of a dangerous mountain climb or sailors in a bad storm at sea. Close to death, you are more alive than at any other time in your life.

In addition, one has to wonder whether today's culture would produce civilian soldiers that could adapt to the extreme conditions encountered in World War II. There were, in fact, relatively few desertions or cases of self-inflicted wounds in spite of the enormous inequity between the number of men serving in the rear echelon compared to the front lines. If you read Will Cavanagh's masterful account of the 99th Division titled "Dauntless," particularly the description of the breakout from the Remagen Bridgehead where small bands of GIs often no more than squads spread out over rough terrain and sought the enemy with such determination, you realize that these ordinary men acted in an extraordinary way. Of course, there was the motivation to put an end to the war, but there was more to it than that because those small bands on the cutting edge knew they were the most exposed to death or serious injury. That self-motivation of the American soldier is perhaps the hardest factor to put your finger on and explain.

This account was not supposed to be a military history. For those who might have interest in looking into what was happening in the sector where most of these experiences occurred, a good start would be the relevant chapters of Charles MacDonald's official military history of the Ardennes Campaign. The best focus is given by J.C. Doherty's extraordinary "The Shock of War" (two volumes, Vert Milon Press) describing what happened along the International Highway and Losheimergraben, and then at Krinkelt, Rocherath, and Elsenborn Ridge. The best appreciation of what the untried, green men of the 99th did in wrecking the timetable of the 6th SS Panzer Army during the first two days of the Bulge can be found in Rusiecki's "Key to the Bulge - The Battle for Losheimergraben" (Praeger).

Because of the ground conditions, the few roads in that part of the Ardennes were the key to success for the German Panzers, and Krinkelt-Rocherath became a funnel that they had to pass through to gain the heights of Elsenborn Ridge, and then get to the Meuse River. After Gen. Robertson, commander of the 2nd Division, was given jurisdiction over the 99th as well, he determined that Krinkelt-Rocherath would be defended as long as feasible, and the twin villages became a death trap for the men and tanks of the Hitler Jugend. The fighting was street by street and from room to room. A look at Doherty's situation maps shows how close to the abyss our battalion was as part of the 395th RCT, but we were lucky.

The Elsenborn sector was the shortest distance from the Meuse River, and it has only been recently, almost half a century after the war, that military writers like Doherty and Rusiecki have demonstrated that the critical battle was there, not at Bastogne, despite all the media hype at the time. There is little interest in that war now, except among the aging population of men and women who served in it, but maybe sometime in the next century groups will organize like the Civil War buffs of today and use virtual reality machines to re-fight the amazing battles of Losheimergraben, Krinkelt-Rocherath, and Elsenborn Ridge.

THE AUTHOR

Francis N. Iglehart was born in Baltimore in 1925 and grew up in the Greenspring Valley area north of the city. He attended Gilman School and then St. Paul's School in Concord, New Hampshire, graduating in 1943, and entering the service a few weeks later. At first, he was assigned to the Army Specialized Training Program (ASTP) unit at Hendrix College in Conway, Arkansas after basic training. With the demise of the ASTP, he was assigned to Company G, 393rd Infantry Regiment of the 99th Infantry Division at Camp Maxey, Texas, going overseas with the Division in September, 1944. Serving as a Browning Automatic Rifleman and assistant squad leader, he was awarded the Purple Heart, Bronze Star, Combat Infantry Badge, and three campaign stars.

After the war, he attended Princeton University on the GI bill and majored in medieval and modern European history, graduating magna cum laude in 1949. He then attended University of Maryland School of Law, entering the practice of law in 1952. At present, he is Of Counsel to the Baltimore law firm of Wright, Constable & Skeen.

Married to the former Harriet Austen Stokes, he is the father of three sons, two daughters, and has three grandchildren. He and his wife live on a farm in the Monkton area of Baltimore County.

Though he has written many legal briefs, this is his first literary endeavor.

Francis N. Iglehart